A Chip and a Prayer

The Duckman's Desperate Quest to Become a Poker Champion

"Marvin Karlins takes you for an entertaining ride deep into the World Series of Poker, and into his 'all-in' effort to capture a coveted WSOP bracelet. From convincing his wife to let him risk $50,000—and spend six weeks in Vegas—to chasing his dream, to his appearance in the main event, the book is clever cover-to-cover!"

Phil Hellmuth Jr., 14-time WSOP winner, *NY Times* best-selling author, and author of the game-changing book, *#POSITIVITY*

"The Duckman is simply one of the most enjoyable people in the poker world. His book is a fun, entertaining read that will keep you smiling throughout. Reading this book should be on your poker bucket list."

Mike Sexton, Poker Hall of Famer, *World Poker Tour* TV Host

"Brilliant, witty and downright hysterical. An inspirational story of defeat and triumph. It's the journey of a brave man who takes a leap of faith to chase a dream, a dream which many share and few follow."

Allison Hollander, Host of the *Bestbet Poker Show*

"Marvin Karlins is a marvelous storyteller making this a must read for those who love poker. Beware: it is funny, devilishly insightful, and a realistically sobering account of what it's really like to be a poker professional. A must read whatever your skill level."

Joe Navarro, Author *What Every BODY is Saying*, *Read 'em and Reap*

"Whether you play poker as an amateur, seasoned professional or are simply an armchair TV fan trying to figure this game out, you will find Karlin's actual account of tournament poker interesting, funny, and most importantly, 100% honest."

Craig Casino: Heartland Poker Tour leading player

"From the very first sentence of *A Chip and a Prayer*, you know you're in the hands of a great writer, a fine storyteller, and a quintessential poker player. So it's a good thing this book is as funny as it is instructive and life-affirming."

Deke Castleman, Author, *Whale Hunt in the Desert*

"I read this book over my vacation and enjoyed every page of it!"

Larry Roberts: Host, *Readily Random Podcasts*

"I had the pleasure of meeting The Duckman when we both made a World Poker Tour final TV table. His book is a fresh perspective on some of the things we all deal with on the tournament scene that will be enjoyed by both the experienced tournament player and the casual observer. This is a fun read for poker fans everywhere."

Stan Jablonski, poker player, actor, businessman

"Written with raw candidness and self-deprecating, wry humor, Karlins shares his poker wisdom and six-week Vegas odyssey of despair and elation, where the turn of a card can make the difference between a dream fulfilled or a nightmare never forgotten."

Dan Ross, Hold'em Media Group

"An honest and transparent amalgamation of Ivy League intellect, poker player snarkyness, and dream-chasing authenticity all wrapped in the wisdom of a man who has 'outlived his life expectancy.'"

Steve Fredlund, Host of the *RecPoker* podcast

"A great read. His account of his ups and downs and the financial costs involved, should be educational and vicariously enjoyable for anyone thinking of embarking on a similar WSOP adventure."

Zachary Elwood, Author *Reading Poker Tells, Exploiting Poker Tells*

A Chip and a Prayer

The Duckman's Desperate Quest to Become a Poker Champion

Marvin Karlins

Cardoza Publishing

DEDICATION

To my mother, Miriam Karlins, a pioneer in the mental health field. Mom championed those who couldn't defend themselves, including my sister, Sandy, who was mentally challenged all her life. I have decided to pledge 25 percent of any tournament winnings and royalties from this book to the mental health facility named in her honor: The Karlins Center in Minneapolis, Minnesota.

And to Edy and Amber, my two pocket aces, forever! They stood by me when the chips were down.

Cardoza Publishing is the foremost gaming publisher in the world, with a library of over 200 up-to-date and easy-to-read books and strategies. These authoritative works are written by the top experts in their fields and with more than 10,000,000 books in print, represent the best-selling and most popular gaming books anywhere.

Front cover photograph by Zeljana Drljaca

Library of Congress Catalog Card No: 2017964678
ISBN: 978-1-58042-367-0

Visit our web site—www.cardozabooks.com—or write
for a full list of books and computer strategies.

CARDOZA PUBLISHING
P.O. Box 98115, Las Vegas, NV 89193
Phone (800) 577-WINS
email: cardozabooks@aol.com

Living the dream,
sweating the nightmares,
and going for broke
at the World Series of Poker

ACKNOWLEDGEMENTS

How can I even begin to thank those individuals who provided me with the insights, friendship and encouragement needed to make this book idea a reality? The answer: "I can't," not adequately, that's for sure. But at least I can recognize them here and say to each one: truly, you were my one-outers that hit on the river!

To Avery Cardoza, my publisher, who had faith in the project and the wisdom to tell me, "Don't quit your day job to play poker."

To Craig Casino, Deke Castleman, Zachary Elwood, Steve Fredlund, Phil Hellmuth Jr., Allison Hollander, Stan Jablonski, Michael Laake, Wally Maddah, Joe Navarro, Dan Ross, Mike Sexton and Anthony Zinno who took the time to review the manuscript and were kind enough not to trash it! Some of their comments are included in the book.

To Linda Johnson, Frankie Jackson, Nick Marts and Robert Ram for their participation in the book cover photoshoot.

To Stan Jablonski, Roger Martin and Derik Melicher who, as top executives at America's Poker Tour, gave me the honor of serving as the Tour's poker ambassador.

To my fellow players in the Tampa Bay Elite Poker League who are on track to become poker legends in their own lifetimes.

To Mike Sexton, Vince Van Patten, Lynn Gilmartin and all the folks with the World Poker Tour who made me feel incredibly special at my final table appearance during the 2015 season.

To the staff and management of the World Series of Poker who did a splendid job of hosting poker's premier event.

And, finally, to Don Delitz, my #1 gambling buddy and all-around great guy. Here's hoping for a few more cross-country road trips to Vegas before I hit that final 7-out.

TABLE OF CONTENTS

PROLOGUE

The Las Vegas Poker Diet
Win at the Poker Table,
Lose at the Dinner Table!

The only difference between a professional
and degenerate gambler is profit or loss.

I am sitting at the intersection of Sun City and Sin City, seat 6, table 70 at the World Series of Poker Super Seniors No-Limit Hold'em tournament. You must be at least sixty-five years old to enter this event, which might explain why there are enough portable oxygen containers scattered about the room to make the casual onlooker think he'd stumbled upon a scuba divers' convention.

All around me competitors in various stages of decay are looking for their seat, some walking as if they are crossing the La Brea tar pits; others seemingly unable to read the table number to which they are assigned.

Hey, the good news is these players are over the hill, not under it. The bad news: A few competitors might not survive long enough to make a decision if someone calls the clock on them. This is probably the one tournament where, when a player busts out, the dealers are instructed to declare "seat open" rather than "player down" because, otherwise, no one will know if the unlucky individual has just experienced a stroke of bad luck or a stroke from clogged arteries.

I scan the cavernous room for portable defibrillators, reminding myself that a casino is the best place to be if you have a heart attack. It's *not* the best place to be, however, if you have thousands of old guys with prostate problems trying to make it to a crowded bathroom after hours of sitting at a poker table.

I shouldn't even be in this tournament. That is the assessment of my wife, as revealed in the following dialogue between us, which I initiated after selecting a romantic setting on the 25th floor balcony of the Cosmopolitan Hotel overlooking the Bellagio fountains along the neon studded Las Vegas Strip.

"Honey, I want to tell you about something I've been thinking of doing."

"Do you think it's wise to give gamblers hotel rooms with access to balconies?"

"Listen, you know I've talked about the fact that I'm not getting any younger, and there's one item on my bucket list I'd really like to cross off."

"Does this have to do with gambling?"

"Well, in fact, it does. How did you know?"

"You're a degenerate gambler…what else would it be about?"

"*Was* a degenerate gambler," I noted. "I play poker now; it's my methadone for overcoming my craps addiction"

"So, what exactly did you have in mind?"

"I want to take the summer off from teaching, spend two months in Vegas, and play the World Series of Poker."

"You *what*?"

I repeated myself.

"I don't think that's a very good idea."

"Why not?"

"Well, for one, you're not that good a poker player."

"Anyone can get lucky and win a tournament," I countered.

"I even beat you heads up!"

"You see, that proves my point. Anyone can win occasionally."

"You told me yourself that players call their friends to get over to the poker room when you sit down to play."

"OK, let's not get testy. It's something I want to do."

"What about your summer salary at the University? You'll be out $25,000."

"That's a good point, but I've saved enough money from my writing and consulting to afford the loss and still have enough funds to play. "And," I added, "none of this money will come from my university income."

"What about a place to stay? That's going to cost more money."

"Already factored in. "A condo will cost $6,000 and I've budgeted for that, too."

"So how much were you planning to gamble?"

"Fifty thousand dollars."

"That's a *lot* of money."

"Good point. "But being willing to gamble $50,000 doesn't mean I'll lose all of it. In fact, I could win—well—*millions!*"

"Putting you in Vegas for two months is equivalent to locking an alcoholic in a liquor store for sixty days."

"It's a challenge I want to face, and conquer. Besides," I added, "I'm not getting any younger. This might be the last chance to live my dream."

"I didn't know you were in a death spiral."

"Last month I asked a poker-playing doctor friend what my life expectancy was. He said I had already exceeded it!"

"You look plenty healthy to me. You'll probably outlive the doctor."

"Even if the doctor is wrong I feel compelled to go. It gives me a sense of purpose and life without purpose is death without dying."

"You can find a less risky, less expensive way to justify your existence," she countered. "Here's the way I see it: Your purpose in life is to take $50,000 in cash and set it on fire."

"That's harsh," I objected, but there wasn't a lot of conviction behind my words. Realistically, I knew I was at the bottom of the food chain when it came to matching my four years of poker experience against the most talented pros in the world. Winning was not impossible—I had made the final table at a WPT televised event just two years ago—but unlikely. I tried to imagine how long it would take to actually burn $50,000.

My wife looked away. Neither of us spoke. We had reached a stalemate of sorts. It was time to play my "sweeten the pot" card. "Listen," I said gently, "I understand your concerns. I even share some of them. But there are other benefits that come with this trip in addition to gambling."

"Such as?"

"Two, in fact. I've signed with a major publisher to write a book about this whole bucket list experience. I could get royalties from that."

"You mean someone is actually *paying* you to write about this stuff?"

"Yes. It's not just a poker journey. I'm including stuff that can help players improve their game."

"So, has it worked for you?"

"Well, I don't always follow my own advice. But when I do, good things can and do seem to happen."

"What's the second benefit?"

"I'm going to use the two months to go on a diet. With all that poker, I figure I won't be as focused on eating or have the time to do so even if I wanted to."

"So now you can lose weight along with your money; isn't that a possible outcome?"

"I'd rather look at it as losing weight and gaining wealth… but, yes, there is a chance I could lose my ass twice!" I pointed at my protruding stomach. "Look, if I don't get this weight off somehow I'm going to end up flying home cargo class. That's assuming I don't die from obesity first. Think of the diet as a health bonus that comes with the gambling package, a kind of Las Vegas poker diet."

Over at the Bellagio the fountains were reaching a climax of sorts, shooting columns of water forty feet in the air. My wife fell silent and watched the spectacle until the final eruption of water faded away and the attraction went dark. Then she turned to walk back inside the room. But before she left the balcony her final words were: "Well,

I don't like it, but I'm not going to deprive you of your dream."

I love my wife!

I'm not a Pollyanna. I harbor no illusions. I know that even the best professional poker players experience *variance,* which is part of the game. This variance means they can run bad for months in a row, or even longer. I also am aware that most full-time players consider themselves successful if they place *in the money,* win prize money, in 15 percent of the tournaments they play. I'll only be playing for six weeks in a limited number of tournaments. Consequently, variance could kill my chances of winning even if I played at the "Phil-Phil" skill level (Hellmuth, Ivey). Plus, I understand the power of *leaks,* a gambling term for players who spend their money at negative expectation games they can't win, craps, for example.

I'm going to be living a few hundred yards from dice tables for two months! One reason I want to share this once-in-a-lifetime journey with each of you, in addition to any educational and enjoyment value it might provide, is because I know I will play better and be less likely to "crap out," knowing my efforts, if unsuccessful, could lead to public humiliation.

The bottom line: When it comes to financial gain, I am a clear underdog. Hell, I'm down $31,000 in costs before I ever get dealt a hand. But that's fine with me. I'm going to bet on myself and take the points.

My wager: I'll cash in at least one tournament in my six weeks of WSOP play. My ultimate goal is to come home with a bigger bankroll than I started with. What happens in Vegas, stays in Vegas, I just don't want it to be *my* money that stays behind. My weight is another matter. My goal is to leave twenty-five pounds in the city known for destroying diets with the ample assistance of celebrity chefs and bountiful buffets beckoning up and down the strip. In sum, I want to win booty and lose booty in my Vegas adventure.

So, let's shuffle up and deal. I've got a chip and a prayer and I'm going for broke, one way or the other!

CHAPTER 1

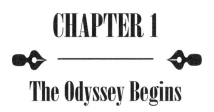

The Odyssey Begins

Revel in the journey or skip the trip.

I decide to drive to Vegas, a journey of 2,350 miles, in my blue bomb, a 2010 Mercury Grand Marquis with a 130,000-mile odometer reading almost double my age. I'm going with my gambling buddy and great guy, Don Delitz. This decision to drive has merit, after all, I've got a lot to pack for a two-month stay and I'll need transportation once I'm out there. But these are not the reasons I chose to drive four long days rather than fly five short hours.

The reason is anticipation. Back in the days when I used to train pilots for Singapore Airlines, I would fly from Changi Airport to LAX (twenty-seven hours) and then drive, rather than fly, to Nevada. I would use this extra time, four hours rather than forty-five minutes, to enjoy anticipation of gambling that was to come. Think about it, once you're in Vegas playing at the tables, the anticipation of all those great possibilities comes to an abrupt halt. Now, you are forced to shift from reverie to reality, and more times than not, that reality is not going to live up to your anticipations.

Best of all, anticipation is free, unlike gambling itself, which can leave little, if any, time for pleasant feelings if you start losing the moment you hit the tables.

Sadly, when I was a dice degenerate, the joy I experienced anticipating the Vegas experience far outweighed the experience itself. I am ashamed to tell you how many times I went on three, four, or five-day junkets to Sin City from my home in Tampa—all expenses paid by the casino—and ended up losing my entire bankroll in the first few hours after I arrived. Not only did I never see my room, I got a taxi back to the airport and returned home on the same airplane I had taken out earlier that morning. Nothing is more pitiful than a gambler who loses his or her bankroll and is left out of action for hours or even days in Vegas. It would be comparable to chaining a starving person to a post, where he could see, but not reach, an endless conveyor belt laden with the finest foods prepared by master chefs.

So, yes, I chose a four-day drive to give me ample time to fantasize about all of the bracelets I would win, how I would invest my six- and seven-figure cashes, and which luxury car I would purchase for the triumphant return home.

Anticipation is the gambler's foreplay! A lover imagines how good things will go in bed; a gambler imagines how good things will go at the tables.

My thoughts drift to Jack Straus, the inspiration behind the title of this book. He was nicknamed "Treetop" because he stood six feet, six inches tall. A high-stakes poker professional, Jack died while playing at the table; toppled over like a giant redwood in the forest, doing what he loved best when the Grim Reaper showed up with the nuts. Jack was best remembered for winning the WSOP main event in 1982 but on his way to victory he played a critical hand where he shoved all his chips into the middle of the pot, was called, and lost.

But wait!

As he got up to leave, a single chip was spotted under his drink napkin. After discussing the situation, the tournament director ruled that because Straus had not declared himself all in, but simply pushed his chips into the middle the one hidden chip was not in play because it had not been part of Treetop's bet.

Straus was allowed to continue playing with the one chip, which as it turned out, was the start of a miracle comeback that culminated in Straus winning the tournament! This incredible turn of events was immortalized in poker lingo as "a chip and a chair," a mantra of enduring hope to every short-stacked poker player who is reminded that victory is possible as long as one has a chip and a chair.

There's also a personal angle to the jack Straus story. Around a decade ago I was playing in a high entry fee (for that time period) poker tournament as a break from a brutal run of crap losses. I was still years away from playing poker on a regular basis, and hardly knew what I was doing. The player on my right was a cordial fellow and doing quite well. During a break in the action, table talk turned to memorable poker events and I mentioned the jack Straus life-support-to- ultimate-comeback-victory in the 1982 main event.

"Wow, can you imagine how the guy must have felt who came in second," I added, and shook my head.

The player next to me physically cringed and said, "I was that guy!" Of course, I thought he was joking, but I was wrong. The guy was Dewey Tomko and he *was* the victim of Jack's improbable comeback. Although I certainly hadn't intended it, my comment effectively put Dewey on tilt and I don't remember him winning another hand the rest of the day.

A chip and a chair. A chip and a prayer. My attitude is set. When it comes to playing in a tournament, if I am in it, I can win it. The spirit of Jack Straus is infused in my body. In my imagination, I am convinced I will win big. Almost a half-century of gambling all comes down to this, a final bucket list item. Take down a major tournament and be a winning gambler for once in my life! I want to savor victory rather than taste defeat.

This is my time. This is my year. This is my chip and a prayer awaiting a positive response!

Sadly, there is no such thing as a guarantee of victory in the cardrooms of Vegas. At least I know my chances will be better than at the dice tables. So, it's Vegas or bust, and hopefully not Vegas and bust. Four days to drive and dream, to immerse myself in what might be. Pinch me when the trip is over.

It's time to shift from driving to win to being driven to win.

CHAPTER 2

●⟡ ———————— ⟡●

I Prepare Myself for Opening Day

If you've played poker on a regular basis for more than three years and haven't learned humility, then you're either extremely lucky, terrifically talented or a certifiable psychopath.

Poker is a game that has been described as taking minutes to learn but a lifetime to master. It is a contest of aggression, competition, and social interaction, a blend of skill and luck. Put simply, it is a microcosm of life itself. And you get to live a new life every time a hand is dealt. Poker tournaments are best described in terms used by pilots to describe their flying careers: "Hours of tedium interrupted by moments of terror."

There are many forms of poker, some that were popular at one time and have all but died-out, others that are up-and-comers and might be the primary choice of future players. However, the current, undisputed favorite form of the game is Texas hold'em poker or, simply, "hold'em."

There are two variations of the game: *limit* hold'em, which restricts the amount of money a player can bet at certain times during the game, and *no-limit hold'em* (NLH), where a player is permitted to bet all the chips or money he has on the table at any time. When playing either form of hold'em, the player has a choice of playing *cash games* (where you can leave the game at any time you wish, hopefully putting your profits in your pockets), and *tournaments*, where players pay a fee to enter ("buy-in") and then must continue playing until they *bust out*, lose all their chips, or the tournament ends, whereupon the prize pool is divided up amongst a given percentage of the winners, normally about 10 to 15 percent of the entrants.

The advantage, in my opinion, of playing tournaments is twofold:

(1) You get more bang for your buck. You usually get more playing time for your money;

(2) You can win a huge amount of money compared to your-buy-in, particularly if there are many entrants to fatten the prize pool.

In my quest to become a poker champion, I have chosen to play, with one exception explained later, no-limit hold'em. I believe this is where I can get the most action, excitement, and potential profit. Also, it is the game most frequently played at the World Series of Poker (WSOP), including the $10,000 main event that caps off the series and is the most coveted victory sought by the thousands of participants who descend on the Rio in Las Vegas every year.

The unique aspect of no-limit hold'em poker tournaments is the sudden death factor involved in the game. Although this factor has been somewhat compromised in recent years with the advent of rebuy and re-entry tournaments, which really make them hybrid cash games, it is still a thrill factor that is hard to duplicate. Because anyone can bet all his or her chips at any time, there is the ongoing possibility with every hand dealt that a player might be knocked out of the tournament. Particularly in multi-day events, where players must survive hundreds of hands to get in the money, it is possible to play perfect poker for ten, twenty hours or even longer, and lose everything you have on one misplayed or unlucky hand. It is brutal. The constant drama of being one hand away from elimination and the fact that good hands can be defeated by inferior ones due to luck—poker players call these *bad beats*—makes tournament play a constant cliffhanger that can create both exhilaration and expletives.

Poker pundits have suggested that to win at the game, it should be viewed as a game of people played with cards. I would suggest that, whether you accept or reject that opinion, winning at poker is intimately connected with the proper psychological frame of mind. The very nature of the game makes the mental aspect of play so critical.

Imagine playing poker tournaments for a living. Sometimes the pressure, competition, hours of concentrated play, bad beats, personality or opinion differences between players, and the fact that even the best tournament poker pros win money less than 20 percent of the time all come together to make one wonder why anyone would voluntarily play the game at all. How many times can a person be content with saying "that's poker" when suffering one horrendous bad beat after another, losing a great hand, say a nut flush, to a better one, like a full house, or ending up on the *bubble*, that is, busting out of the tournament, just short of the money?

One of my friends claimed that Florida opened the poker rooms after they shut down the mental hospitals. Maybe he's on to something. It seems you'd have to be crazy, or a masochist, to play such a nerve-shattering game. Yet, for those of us who love poker, the game is an ultimate high, a feeling of exhilaration rarely duplicated in other forms of behavior. What is critical, of course, is to play well enough to win, and, hopefully, the following suggestions will help you steadily grow your poker bankroll.

For those readers who are not familiar with no-limit hold'em poker, I have provided an explanation of how it is played in Appendix A. Please read that material now; it will make the rest of the book more understandable and enjoyable. Ditto for no-limit hold'em tournaments. If you don't understand how such events work, check out Appendix B before we get into the action in later chapters.

Getting psychologically prepared to play your A game——playing in the zone.

Winning or losing in poker is dependent on three things:

(1) The cards you are dealt.

(2) The opponents you face.

(3) Yourself. The serenity prayer provides valuable insight on how to correctly approach the game.

> *Grant me the serenity to accept*
> *the things I cannot change,*
> *courage to change the things I can,*
> *and the wisdom to know the difference.*

We can't choose which cards we will receive, and, controlling our opponents is extremely difficult, and in some cases, impossible, which leaves you as the one thing that can be controlled. Players who can control themselves at the poker table have a definite edge over those who can't. Here is what you can do to put yourself in the best possible psychological frame of mind to help you realize your full potential as a player and perform your best once the cards are in the air.

(1) Follow the "BMW" approach to drive yourself to victory.
Just as it is easier to eat a large piece of meat if you cut it into smaller pieces so, too, is a poker tournament easier to win if you break it down into three stages (or goals).

B (Bag Some Chips).
The first thing I strive to do in a multi-day tournament, which most big-money tournaments are these days, is focus on making it through Day 1 and bagging chips for the next day of play. I refer to a popular poker maxim. "You can't win a multi-day tournament in the first day, but you can definitely lose it." My goal is to steadily accumulate chips and, hopefully, have at least the average-size chip stack to bag for later play.

M (Get in the Money).
Once you've bagged chips, your next goal is to use them to get in the money. In most multi-day tournaments, you must get past between 25 to 50 percent of the remaining Day 2 competitors to reach the payout level, and that's what you want to shoot for. Nothing is more demoralizing than playing a day and a half of poker, anywhere from

fifteen to twenty hours and longer, and getting knocked out short of the money. Bubbling a tournament—being the last player to be eliminated before payouts begin—is one of the worst feelings a poker player can experience. Getting in the money involves adjusting your play in a manner that increases the chances of a payout.

W (Go for the Win).

Once you're in the money, it's time to set your sights on reaching the final table and winning the tournament. That is the ideal outcome. A more reasonable goal is to shoot for a finish in the top three spots, where over a third of the money is awarded. Anytime you reach the final table of a multi-day tournament, you are talking about big payouts.

(2) Focus on being the best you can be, not the best there is, when it comes to playing poker.

In other words, I try to play to my maximum potential and not worry about whether some other player is better than I am. You don't have to be the best poker player in the tournament to win it. If you set your goal at being the best there is, at anything, rather than being the best you *can* be, you are very likely to face disappointment. Poker is not chess. On any given day, or in any given tournament, any poker player, regardless of his or her talent and experience, can be beat. Don't waste your energy wondering if your opponent is so good he is unbeatable. He's not! When you stop focusing your attention on the strength of your opposition and concentrate on playing your best "A" game, you'll be giving yourself the best possible shot at victory.

28

(3) Try not to make mistakes, but when you do, put them behind you and move forward.

Every poker player is going to make mistakes. It is a given. The real tragedy is when a player makes a mistake and then compounds it with a second mistake, that is, letting that initial mistake affect future play. Poker players call this mental breakdown, *going on tilt*. If you make a mistake, it helps to remember that even the greatest players make them, too. Every time I make a mistake, I simply remember the time Phil Ivey, considered by many as the greatest player in the game, *mucked*, threw away, a winning flush on national television—and then I get back to my game.

(4) Never play poker unless your desire to do so is strong!

Poker is a hard way to make easy money. Even the best players lose far more often than they win. The hours are long. The nature of the game itself, with the luck factor thrown in, can lead to excruciating losses. Mike Sexton, the nationally televised announcer of WPT fame, nailed it in his book, *"Life's a Gamble,"* when he said:

> "I always tell anyone who is thinking about becoming a professional player that even if you have the talent to do it and are a winning player, if you don't love to play poker—not like to play, but *love* to play—don't do it because you'll be miserable."

Unless I am really enthused to play, I won't. It's that simple. I suspect that if I played poker for a living I'd probably end up with a severe case of burnout.

> **TIPS & QUIPS: TIP #1**
> A friend once asked me if I made a living playing
> poker and I said: "I make a life playing poker." If you
> love the game, you'll understand the distinction.

You know how you feel when you've eaten far more than
you should have at the local buffet? That bloated stomach, the queasy feeling, the mental image of a stuffed tur-
key you can't ignore? You can overindulge in poker, too.
Each person has their poker limit, when the game can't
hold your interest and your passion. When that limit is
reached, it's time for a break from the tables. I've never met a successful poker player who is bored with the
game. Seasoned pros know the signs of burnout and will
take a break from the tables to rejuvenate their bodies and
passion for the game when their joy for playing wanes.
Those that don't usually end up either broke or in some
other line of work.

(5) Recognize that great tournament players can't be afraid to take risks.
This psychological behavior is well-described by my
friend Steve, who went to a circus and watched a performer do all kinds of fancy acrobatics as he walked a
high wire between platforms set forty feet off the ground.
A few weeks later my friend visited a different circus and
saw a different high-wire act. This time, the performer
simply walked across the thin wire, using a long pole to
keep his balance. Yet, Steve was much more impressed
with him than the acrobatic first performer.

Why? Because the second performer, unlike the first,
didn't use a safety net. If he fell he faced severe injury or

death, and Steve appreciated the risk the performer was taking to entertain him.

If you want to be a successful no-limit hold'em player, you have to be a risk-taker. You can't worry about falling, about building safety nets. There's no room for the faint-of-heart, risk-aversive performer in no limit poker! When money becomes anything more than a method of keeping score, you're dead.

(6) It is good to feel confident at the tables, but self-pride can be a killer. Whenever I am asked to draw the line between constructive confidence and destructive pride, I'm reminded of an incident involving the gambling whale Kerry Packer. Before he passed away, Packer was an Australian tycoon who regularly bet $10 to $20 million a weekend on gambling junkets around the world. One day, while gambling high-limit baccarat at Caesars Palace, he became disturbed by a foul-mouthed gambler who was playing at his table and cursing the dealers for his bad luck.

Eventually, Kerry's patience wore thin, and he politely asked the player to stop behaving so rudely. That made the loser even more abrasive, and he told the Australian, "Listen, buddy, you obviously don't know who you're talking to. I happen to be worth more than $40 million dollars!"

Upon hearing this claim, Packer casually replied, "I'll flip you for it."

"Pride!" You can't be prideful and be a winner at the poker table. Confident, yes; prideful, no! Pride can cloud your judgment and put you on tilt. Pride can make you play over your head rather than with it. It can make you beat yourself. Humility is a poker player's winning hand; never forget that "pride goeth before the fall"

(7) When you're ahead, know when to quit!

Early in my gambling career, I was in Vegas with a husband and wife who were my friends. After a particularly dismal gambling session, we all headed to the elevator to call it a night. Or so I thought. Once the elevator doors closed, my two friends got in a heated argument. The husband told his wife, "Give me back the money I told you not to give me."

At first, his wife steadfastly refused, already furious about her husband's casino losses. Finally, however, she relented and said in disgust, "Here is your damn thousand. Just take it and leave me alone, I'm going to bed."

At this point, the wife got off the elevator and the husband nodded to me. "Let's head downstairs and get our money back," he said resolutely. It was 11:00 PM.

Some five hours later, my married friend had enjoyed a massive *heater*, running the original $1,000 into $80,000 at the baccarat table. Four more hours passed, and he lost it all, including the initial $1,000. His entire bankroll was gone! There was nothing left to do but go back upstairs to his room, where he was met at the door by his wife.

"Well?" she asked, "how did you do?"

"I lost the $1,000," the husband replied without hesitation.

Which was technically true and probably saved Vegas from recording another homicide. Just don't you be the gambler that eats like a bird (bets small) when he's winning and shits like a moose (bets big) in an attempt to get his losses back. Most important: Don't go for the chandeliers. When you're winning at poker, especially cash games, know when to walk away a winner. It's what separates the victors from the vanquished.

(8) Don't gamble with money you can't comfortably afford to lose.
There's an old gambling story that's been circulating for years. It always gets a laugh, but don't let the humor hide the severe problem it identifies. A guy goes to his friend's house and wants to borrow $400. When the friend asks him why he needs the cash, the man explains he is desperately low on funds and faces loss of electricity and maybe even eviction if he can't come up with the rent money. Feeling sorry for his buddy, the homeowner goes into his bedroom, fetches four hundred-dollar bills, and hands them over. The borrower takes out his wallet and shoves the cash inside, thanking his new creditor as he does so.

But wait! As the man opens his wallet, the lender sees several Benjamins already nestled there.

"Hold on a minute," he says with surprise, "I thought you said you didn't have enough money to pay your bills. What about that cash in your wallet?"

"Oh, *that*. That's gambling money," explains the man who had requested the loan.

I call degenerate/compulsive/addictive gambling the *termite disease*, because you often don't discover it until the house is ready to collapse. Gamblers should never be betting money they can't afford to lose. Not only can it affect his or her quality of play, it can also affect a person's quality of life. When you bet money you *have* to win, it affects your decision-making, you take risks when you shouldn't and don't when you should. It's simple, really. Scared money never wins in the long term.

*****

I run through the eight points I just described before every tournament I play. I know that, if I follow these playing strategies, I will significantly increase my chances to win gelt on the felt. If I don't feel mentally ready, I know my best option is to skip the tournament and wait to play until I have the proper psychological edge on my side of the table.

Tonight, on the eve of my first tournament, is no different. I decide to go over my eight-point strategy while getting some fresh air by taking a walk on the Strip. The moment I step outside, I take pleasure in soaking up the kinetic energy radiating from the neon dazzle that stokes the nervous system like a hit of epinephrine. Some locals dislike the Strip and avoid it like the plague. Not me. In my mind, the Strip is ground zero of the American Dream and I am awash in the electric energy that bombards my senses.

Up and down the street, the juggernaut casinos wait like armed men, their huge neon bludgeons flashing against the desert sky. "It's like running a damn gauntlet," my friend's father used to warn as he drove us down the Strip. "Just look at those casinos lining each side of the street, ready to beat you out of your money. Just how long do you think you can run the gauntlet without losing your shirt?"

His point was well-taken. I have felt the sting of turning my pants' pockets inside out, the gambler's white flag of surrender. But tonight, I convince myself, old losses don't matter. This moment marks the eve of a new beginning, a new chance, a new hand dealt my way. A winning hand.

Beginning tomorrow I will not be just another Las Vegas loser. This will be my summer of Vegas victory!

I hope.

CHAPTER 3

Spring Training: Can David Beat Goliath?

**If I don't play poker for more than a week, I begin hallucinating.
The last time it happened, I saw an ace Hardware next to a
Burger king and wondered if they were suited.**

I left Tampa for Vegas on May 10th, arrived on the 15th, spent a week with my wife, and, now, it's May 25th· and I'm finally going to see a hand of poker! The wait is interminable. I have decided to get ready for my WSOP season with a bit of Spring Training at the Planet Hollywood's $250,000 Goliath deep-stack no-limit hold'em tournament.

I'm so excited I hope I don't have premature jacks elation!

This tournament promises to provide some much-needed playing time. In fact, the tournament structure requires thirteen hours of play on Day 1 just to get to the final day, assuming, of course, you still have chips after seventeen 40-minute playing levels. With a 15-minute break every two hours, and one 30-minute dinner break, this tourney will be a test of endurance, kidney control and hunger management.

Tips & Quips: Tip #2: "Sock it to Them!"

Perhaps some of you are familiar with the medical condition called "deep vein thrombosis." Having spent twenty years traveling between Florida and Singapore (twenty-seven hours of flying one way). I learned about this affliction from pilots who had to sit for long hours in the cockpit. Sitting for extended periods of time increases the chances that a person will develop a blood clot which, if it travels to certain vital organs, can be fatal.

Poker players who sit long hours at the tables in tournaments like the Goliath increase their risk of deep vein thrombosis. One simple and effective way to reduce your chances of falling victim to this affliction is to wear compression socks throughout the tournament. They can be purchased at most drug stores or online. Check with your doctor about the size and compression level socks that are right for you. A special bonus: When you wear the socks, you'll be amazed how refreshed your legs will feel the next day. I noticed a remarkable reduction in leg cramps as well.

The Tourney Journey Begins: May 25, 2017

I arrive at Planet Hollywood a half hour before the tournament and valet park. I find out that such an option is no longer free, it's $13 for the first four hours and $18 for the day. Luckily, I have my Total Rewards card (an affinity card that casinos give their regular customers who gamble) and discover that allows me to avoid the charge. So, I'm already up $18 (not counting the thousands of dollars in losses it cost me to "earn" the card).

I go to the poker room and find out the tournament isn't being played there but, rather, upstairs, on the second floor, above the casino. I remind myself that it's not only important to get to a tournament with time to spare so you don't feel agitated and rushed when you sit down; you need to know where the tournament venue is as well.

Almost all casino tournaments these days require that you have an affinity card from their casino to enter the tournament. This is another thing a player needs to remember: Getting an affinity card can be a time-consuming process, it's not something you want to go through if you're on a tight schedule. At any rate, after providing my card, driver's license, and $600 entry fee, I'm given my table and seat number which is randomly generated by the computer. I prefer to sit next to the dealer or in the 4, 5, 6 or 7 seats, because otherwise I have trouble seeing the community cards dealt face up in the center of the table.

However, I am assigned seat 3. So much for good sight-lines!

The tournament starts promptly and I find myself playing with only four other opponents at the table. This is yet another factor to consider in a player's poker equation. If you play the first level of a tournament you will often do so with your table half full or less. This means that blinds come around more quickly and this changes the playing dynamic. I know of many pros who purposely don't show up until the second or third level of a multi-level tournament to avoid this very problem. If you use this strategy, remember not to buy your ticket in advance, otherwise, your stack will be put into play at the outset of the tournament, and you will be blinded off as if you were actually playing. This won't happen if you buy your seat once the tournament has started, you will start with a full stack of chips.

The fact that my table is short-handed doesn't faze me. I'm rarin' to play. My first opportunity to bet comes after only five hands are dealt. I peek at my hole cards, see an ace jack unsuited, and make a 3x bet (three times the big blind of $100). I get one caller. When a jack comes on the flop I bet $1,000 and my opponent mucks his hand. I've won my first tournament hand!

Sweet! I'm ahead for the summer!

Play continues and the table fills up. I win a few hands and lose a few hands, nothing dramatic for the first three levels. After a 20-minute break I come back and am dealt a pair of tens. I bet $1,000, the button raises to $5,000, and I three-bet him to $10,000. He folds. My chip stack is beginning to look robust. A half hour later, I pick up a K-Q unsuited in a hand that's checked around. The flop comes K-J-8 *rainbow*, three cards, all of different suits, and I bet $5,000. One opponent calls, everyone else folds. The turn is a 3♥. I bet $10,000 and my opponent raises me to $20,000! I call, and we both check the river card of 9. I flip over my two kings, and my opponent mucks his hand. I have now doubled my starting chip stack, and I begin fantasizing about a final table finish.

At the end of nine levels of play, we take a thirty-minute break to *race off* the $25 chips, exchange lower denomination chips for higher ones with the odd leftover chips, awarded to players dealt the highest cards, and get dinner. I am sitting on almost $90,000. Sadly, after dinner, it was

I who was eaten alive. Usually, in a major tournament, you can look back on one hand that was a turning point in how you finished, and this one was mine. I got it all in with queens against an opponent who called with a pair of sevens. I'm almost a 5-1 favorite to win the hand and double up to almost $200,000. The dealer turns over three cards, all spades. I look at my queens, both red. I look at my opponent's cards, one red diamond and one black spade. My chances are still good, but now my opponent's odds have improved. He is about a 3-1 underdog to complete his flush.

The turn is the 10♠, and, just like that, I'm history. From the penthouse to the outhouse, as they say.

A bad beat? Yes. But I've seen a lot worse. I shrug my shoulders get up from the table, and congratulate my opponent, who says he's sorry. Neither of us mean it. "That's poker," I add, the comment of choice to make after a *suck-out*, a big underdog hand that draws out to win.

I do my walk of shame out the door. The dealer has the decency to wait until I'm well away from the table before exclaiming "Seat open."

Because there are three Day-1s scheduled for this event, I decide to shoot a second bullet on the 26th of May. Now, I have $1,200 invested and know the only way I can recover it will be with a finish in the top 10 percent of the players receiving payouts. I usually don't like to fire more than one bullet per tournament, as it seems to me that rebuys/re-entries defeat the whole notion of the tournament format. I much prefer freeze-out contests where once you are out, you're out for good.

I know some players who will shoot two, three, four bullets, or even more, in a single tournament. Just to win their money back, they'd have to finish in the top three or four places, but they put up the extra buy-ins anyway. They've got the money, and some of them purposely play recklessly, hoping to double up by getting lucky and then play normally with a double chip stack. Poker pro Daniel Negraneau is famous for this multiple buy-in tactic. He once bought in forty-eight times to a WSOP $1,000 no-limit hold'em bracelet event. Obviously, this tactic makes a mockery of a tournament format, but that's a rant I will save for another day.

Daniel is not the only multiple-entry tournament player. I personally know a doctor who owns a string of medical clinics in Tampa, who bought in over twenty times during a $300-entry tournament. I played against him once when he purchased another entry with 1:47 minutes left before the rebuy period ended. With one hand to go before the break, a young lady who had carefully built her original $20,000 stack to almost double that amount, opened the final hand with a raise. The doctor shoved all his newly purchased chips in the middle of the table and announced, "All in."

> **Tips & Quips: Quip # 1**
> Tournament wisdom: If you're cashing tournaments but losing money, you might want to admit you have a rebuy problem. "If at first you don't succeed, rebuy again" is not necessarily a winning strategy

The young woman called, and turned over A-Q suited. The doctor flipped his cards face up as well, an unsuited

10-5. Everyone knew what was coming. The flop was 10-5-2. The doctor's two pair held up, the woman lost half her stack, and the physician doubled up.

I sometimes wonder what might happen if this doctor fires so many bullets and still loses. Do the costs of his cat scans go up the next day?

May 26, 2017: Bullet Two, Goliath $250,000/$600 Buy-in

I decide to call this second-shot "my day of redemption," and vow to bag. I make one big, aggressive-looking stack of my chips, figuring that height makes might." My opponents don't seem intimidated, and, within two levels, I'm down to $17,000 from my original $30,000 stack. I'm starting to wonder if I'll ever bag, let alone be in the money or a final table. A comment I made to a fellow player when he was running bad comes back to haunt me:

TIPS AND QUIPS: QUIP #2

The best way to assure yourself a seat at a final table is to become a dealer.

Then along comes a critical hand, the kind that I mentioned earlier, that can propel you to the final table or out the door. I get all of my remaining chips in with K-K against pocket jacks and double up. Now, I'm back above starting stack level, and I began getting some decent hands to play. Over the next five levels, I build my stack at a moderate pace but am still in danger of tapping out should I lose one big hand. Then, two things happen that help me maintain my chip stack and end up propelling me into the Day 2 finals. The fact that one thing has nothing to do with my poker playing and the other everything to do with my poor poker playing illustrates how winning poker tournaments can happen due to a confluence of factors, some that are not discussed in poker books, and others that, if they were, you wouldn't want your name associated with them.

The first thing that happened involved the posting of my blinds. It was late in the tournament, Level 16, the next to last level for Day 1, and each round of blinds costs the players $6,000 ($2,000 small blind, $4,000 big blind). Just before I was due to put in my big blind, I was moved to another table, where I ended up between the small and big blind. Thus, I was required to sit out one hand and not pay any blinds for a full round at my new table, plus having played an entire round at my old table and not having to post the blinds there, either. So, basically, at a critical time—when bagging was only one level away, and I was relatively short on funds—I was able to save $12,000 in blinds while getting two full rounds of cards.

The second thing that happened illustrates that sometimes a dumb or, more politely stated, wrong decision can actually end up helping, rather than hurting your chances to win a hand. In my case, it was a simple case of misreading my hole cards. I thought they were the 7♠ and 8♠, and when the flop came 3-3-8 rainbow I called an opponent's moderate bet. When the turn produced a 6♦, I felt my eights were good. Because I was first to act, I made a good-sized bet, and my opponent folded. I took a last look at my cards before throwing them away, and, to my horror, discovered that my suited connectors were not 8-7 but, rather, 7-6. Had I read my hand correctly I would have tossed away the 7-6 when my opponent bet the flop, but I didn't do so because I thought I had the top pair on the board. Am I proud I won the hand this way? No. Am I happy I won the hand this way? Do lottery players throw away their winning tickets? That hand ended up being the last one I played that day and helped me bag $85,000 for the Day 2 finals and a shot at getting in the money.

May 28, 2017: Day 2: Goliath $250,000/$600 Event

If you'll recall, earlier in the book, I stated that one of my major objectives was to finish in the money in at least one tournament. Now I had a shot of achieving this objective in my first tournament! Well, that kind of kills the mystery and the motivation of the project, so I made a command decision before sitting down to play. Because this was a spring training tournament, it shouldn't count in the final standings for the book, especially since it wasn't a WSOP event. So, win or lose, it would not affect "regular season" action.

Nevertheless, you can bet the ranch I wanted to make it to the prize pool in the worst way!

When I saw the final day standings, I didn't think I had much of a chance to reach my goal. Out of the 391 players who had entered the tournament, 61 remained. I was in 51st place. Normally, I'd have to get through half of those players to cash, about 50 percent of the remaining field. But my assessment changed when it was announced that 45 players would be paid. That cut the percentage down to 25 percent—a realizable goal.

I could sense that this might be my day when I got a break before the first hand was dealt. I had initially been as-signed a seat next to the tournament leader (with over

$600,000 in chips), but a minute before play was to start, the tournament director broke our table and I was moved to a new one where I was surrounded by less imposing chip stacks. Then, ten minutes into the action, I was moved again to an even more favorable table. Three different tables in ten minutes. It's the first time I've ever left a table twice in ten minutes and not done so because I was knocked out of the tournament!

When I finally got settled in at my third table, I won two hands in one rotation, once when I raised with A-3 in late position and everyone folded and once when I went all-in with pocket tens against an early raise and my opponent folded. This helped me build my stack over the six-figure mark, where it was slowly whittled away by the blinds and antes ($13,500 a round). I was fast becoming a victim of the "Broomcorn's Uncle" effect, Doyle Brunson's way of saying that, if you don't bet, you'll suffer chip depletion, courtesy of the blinds and antes, yet I was confident that I had enough chips to get in the money and was determined to play only premium hands.

I actually considered leaving the table and not coming back until everyone was in the money, but I decided that wasn't a Real Poker Player's option.

I didn't get any premium hands, but I did make the money! With roughly a half hour left in the third round of play (Level 20: ante $1,000, blinds $5,000/$10,000) the bubble burst and I was a tournament money-winner in Las Vegas! At this point my chip stack was the smallest at the table, but I was able to nurse it to a 36th place finish. With approximately $20,000 left, I went all-in on my big blind and lost when my J-10 unsuited lost to ace high.

I left the table smiling so widely I thought I'd get a facial cramp. My payout of $1,245 more than covered my two $600 entry fees; in fact, I won (trumpets, please)—$45! Given that I played twenty levels at 40 minutes per level, that totals 800 minutes or 13.33 hours, an average win of $3.40 per hour. After leaving an additional tip for the dealers, my "take-home" pay dropped under $2.00. Then there's taxes.

I'm not quitting my day job just yet!

> **TIPS & QUIPS: QUIP #3**
> If someone tells me making a living playing poker is easy, I know they haven't tried or they're a liar.

May 29, 2017: Final Evening of Spring Training:

After my underwhelming win in the Goliath tourney I wasn't intending to play any more poker until it counted, specifically the WSOP's multi-day Colossus which was beginning June 2. With names like "Goliath," "Colossus," "Giant," and "Monster Stack," I figured I should save my strength for what lay ahead. However, earlier in the day I talked with Derek Melicher, president of America's Poker Tour. He wanted to give me my official badge as the tour's ambassador, and I planned to wear it during all of my future play.

He suggested we meet and play a $130 tourney at Planet Hollywood while we were there. There was also an "all in or fold" tournament being played as well, a unique twist on the game allowing the player only two decisions, go all in with their hand, or fold it.

I arrived late for the $130 tournament, and, against my own advice, decided to play anyway. Forced to bet quickly or get blinded out, I was forced to play hands I normally would have folded and ended up losing all my chips.

Down $130, I registered for the "all in or fold" tourney and ended up with nothing. Now I'm down $230 and slightly on tilt. I register again for the "all in or fold" challenge and this time win three bounties ($25 dollars for each person you knock out of the tournament) before being KO'd myself. This brought my night's losses to $255.

Even though I lost the $255, I was glad I played in the tournaments because it underscored an important point that I intend to keep forefront in my mind once the WSOP season gets underway: Don't play in tournaments on the spur of the moment or buy in after four levels have been played. In the former case you're not mentally prepared to do your best, and in the latter situation your starting chips are often too limited to give you a comfortable number of big blinds to play your best game. This is particularly true in many WSOP events, where starting chip stacks are very low, when compared to the deep stack tournaments being played at other venues.

I also experienced something for the first time in my poker career, a dealer error that cost me a critical hand in the $130 tournament. The hand played out this way: I had a K-J against my opponent's unknown cards. He raised before the flop and I called. The flop came K-rag-rag ("rag" is an insignificant card) and I made a sizeable bet. My opponent snap-called all in, and I obliged by doing the same. We turned over our cards. My two kings turned out to be a big dog against my opponent's pocket aces.

The turn card was inconsequential and then, on the river, lightning struck. A second king hit the board, giving me trip kings over my challenger's aces. I had won on a two-outer!

Or so I thought.

One of the player's pointed to the dealer and said, "You forgot to burn a card before you dealt the river."

Sure enough, after checking the cards in front of her, it became clear that the king I received should have been the burn card rather than the miracle winner that would have landed me a boatload of chips. The floor was called, and, sadly, I already knew what the ruling was going to be. The dealer was instructed to remove the king and deal the next card off the top of the deck as the new river card.

No, it wasn't the case king.

Talk about going from elation to dejection in less than sixty seconds. I wasn't a happy camper, but what could I do? Dealers make mistakes just like everyone else; it just had never impacted me in the past. My major consolation is that it was only a $130 tournament.

I am sure the error would have haunted me the rest of my life had it taken place in the WSOP main event.

CHAPTER 4

It's World Series Time, Baby!
Game On!

Covering the World Series of Poker is a reporter's dream...and why not?
We journalist scout the globe for human interest stories and it turns
out that the Binion folks have a surefire recipe for cooking up
such tales right here at home! Here's their formula:
(1) Place in one room approximately 200 of the most colorful
personalities on this earth.
(2) Mix these individuals together with liberal amounts of money and season
with a pinch of pressure and a dash of desire.
(3) Let them simmer slowly over a poker table for approximately four days.
(4) When fully cooked, remove whoever is left and interview
them while they are still warm.

I wrote the statement you just read when I was covering the WSOP in 1992 as a senior editor and columnist for the now defunct *Gambling Times* magazine. It appeared as a quote in the *World Series of Poker* magazine that the Horseshoe used to publish every year. Although the statement is a quarter-century old and some things have evolved (change 200 personalities to 7,000, four days to ten and remove the Binion reference) the majority of what I said back then remains equally true today.

The World Series of Poker is the ultimate proving ground for every aspiring poker player; and the main event bracelet is the most coveted prize in the game. It has also grown into the richest sporting/entertainment event in the world, with seventy-four bracelet events and total cash prizes in the tens of millions of dollars. The winner of the main event can expect to walk away with between $6 million to $9 million, plus endorsements that result in additional money and stardom. (In 2006, at the height of poker's popularity, Jamie Gold won the main event and collected a record $12 million for his achievement.)

To anyone who has never actually attended a WSOP event, the scene of a cavernous ballroom filled with hundreds of poker tables can be, simply, overwhelming. Throw in the color and drama created by placing a few thousand poker players in one contained space, along with the electric Vegas atmosphere that adds sizzle to the experience, and you end up with a spectacle that challenges the human mind to take it all in.

And I'm right in the center of it. Yes! Not as a reporter, but as a player with $50,000, ready to go into battle.

One could make an argument that other tournaments in town provide better value for the money. With lower casino rakes, the money taken out of your entry fee to pay the house for staging the event, larger starting stacks, and great prize guarantees, places like the Venetian, Aria, Wynn, planet Hollywood, and Golden Nugget offer tempting alternative venues to invest one's poker bankroll. The reason I have chosen to play WSOP events has more to do with history and prestige than value, structure and starting chip stacks. As the oldest and most recognized poker tournament in the world, winning a WSOP bracelet is the gold standard of poker excellence.

Capturing the main event bracelet can make you a household name.

In short, if I want to play poker on my field of dreams, I want it to be the premium piece of poker turf on Earth. And every six weeks in the summer, that real estate—the epicenter of the poker world—is located just a few blocks from the strip at the Rio Hotel and Casino.

Before I begin my first day of WSOP play I want to make one final observation. In the past, poker tournaments were freeze-out affairs. Under this format, you were allowed to buy in to the tournament once and, if you lost your chips, that was it. You were done. Finished. You couldn't buy back into the tournament and take another shot at winning.

This freeze-out format was true tournament poker and the staple of the WSOP for decades. In the 2017 tournaments, fifteen of the seventy-four WSOP bracelet events (over 20 percent) are now rebuy or re-entry tournaments, making them basically hybrid cash games. Hopefully, the main event will forever remain a freeze-out as a real tournament was meant to be.

From Goliath to Colossus
Opening day!

The first day of my WSOP season is a lot like the start of baseball season. This is when hopes of making the money or even the playoffs to a championship bracelet springs eternal, like the perennials that bloom in May as each new WSOP begins. I am hyped, psyched and doing what I like!

The first major tournament on the WSOP schedule is the Colossus, a multi-day affair that guarantees a $1 million prize along with a bracelet. Because of the massive number of players involved in the tournament, over 18,000 in total, there are six chances spread over three days to enter the tournament, plus the option of six rebuys, giving the persistent punter the opportunity to fire twelve bullets in pursuit of a Colossus victory. Because of the huge prize potential, the low number of starting chips (only $5,000) and the relatively cheap price to play ($565), the conditions were perfect to encourage multiple entries and rebuys. I hoped I wouldn't have to use the rebuy option.

Colossus: Strike One
I arrive at the Rio a full two-hours early, primarily because I want to soak in the WSOP vibe that resonates throughout the massive convention center area at the back of the hotel, which has been transformed into poker's Ground Zero for the next six weeks. I hear three bad beat stories before I even get through the parking lot, up the stairs, and into the building.

It is over 100 degrees outside, but inside is a blazing poker inferno! It's like a carnival midway on steroids, with people rushing about to get on their "ride" (the seat at their table) and all kinds of vendors selling everything poker, from personalized chips to tax advice. There are also some unique body treatments on sale, from the mundane, like massages, to the outlandish, such as a cylinder which appears to be a cross between an iron lung and a washing machine, where a person's body is pounded by high powered jets of water while laying inside a plastic cylinder. I pause for a moment to study a guy who is enclosed in the wash cycle of the cylinder, his arms sticking out, and his body wrapped in some rubber-like substance. I wonder if this device is on loan from Gitmo.

Fifty feet away there is a row of people sitting on bar stools inhaling unknown fumes from multi-colored tanks of liquid. I consider trying it but decide that having two prongs stuck into my nostrils might not be that enjoyable. I also wonder if the prongs are thrown away or sanitized and reused. I decide not to ask the young lady tending the booth, who is busy massaging a man's head with a wire device that slides up and down his scalp like a metal octopus opening and shutting its tentacles.

Further down the hallway, as I approach the main playing area, an attractive woman approaches me. Given my age, physical condition, and face only your pet would kiss I know something was for sale. It turns out she is hawking some type of French-made energy boosting pills. I thank her and promise that, if I need more energy, I will stop back and see her. Right now, however, my energy is through the roof, and I would prefer a dose of Valium rather than vitality.

I had already purchased my seat online the day before, paying just under $20 for the convenience. It turns out to be a great investment, as the registration line to buy into the tournament is longer than the one at Wal-Mart just before the doors open on Black Friday. The poker dream is alive and well at the Rio.

My seat assignment is in the Amazon room, the largest of the Rio poker rooms. Huge pictures of past main-event winners are hung from the walls, and I can't help but wonder if the early pioneers like Johnny Moss (a three-time winner) could ever, in their wildest moments of imagination, foresee what the WSOP would become. My table is in the shadow of Stuey Unger's photo, the only other player to win the main event three times. Many argue that Stuey was the greatest hold'em player ever (nobody disputed his #1 status as the greatest gin player), yet he died penniless and prematurely in a seedy motel room from drug usage and other personal problems. Although I believe the medical examiner listed the cause of death as "heart failure," a more proper diagnosis may have been "death by lifestyle."

As I take my seat, staring at Unger's youthful image puts me in a somber mood. Having dealt with addiction (gambling) myself, I can empathize with Stuey's struggles, how he had battled his personal demons and lost. If you have any weaknesses, Vegas will find them and put you to the test. I decide to think of Stuey's photo the next time I approach a crap table. I figure it will help keep things in the right perspective.

All around the room, large tournament clocks are set at 30:00, indicating the time of the first blind level. To get through the day will require surviving eighteen levels, or nine hours of play. Because of the tournament format, where blinds and antes are constantly increasing with each new level, a player can't just sit and wait for premium hands to play. This is particularly true in today's event where you only get $5,000 in starting chips. For example, if you played and won just enough to maintain your $5,000 stack for two hours, then you would enter Level 5 (ante $50, blinds $150/$300) with each round of play costing you almost 20 percent of your stack. To further illustrate how you must keep playing and winning to stay in contention for surviving the day, consider that by Level 12 (two-thirds through Day 1 play) it will cost you slightly under your original buy-in of $5,000 just to play one round of poker—$2,400 in blinds and $2,000 in antes at a ten-player table.

I suspect that the Colossus will become a colossal shove-fest in a very short period of time. I give the dealer my driver's license and entry slip and I get, in return, three yellow $1,000 chips, three pink $500 chips, four black $100 chips and four green $25 chips. Looking at the feeble number of chips, I feel like I've already lost 75 percent of my stack, and this is before the first hand is dealt! Although a full table contains ten competitors and the dealer, at the outset of a tournament not every seat is filled. In fact, WSOP rules state that, once the tournament starts, any table with two (sometimes four) or more players can begin play.

This is one reason I don't like sitting down at the table for the first round. There is too much of a chance the table will be only half full, meaning that the blinds will be coming around far more frequently than at a full table. But with a $5,000 starting stack, I have no choice. I can't wait too long; once the blinds go up, my small starting stack will be even more vulnerable to depletion.

One of my goals for my first tournament was to win the first hand I played in.

I didn't.

The second goal was to bag chips and move on to Day Two.

I didn't.

When I finally lost my last chips, making the obligatory shove with my namesake hole cards (2-2), I went out in Level 9, placing 570th out of 2,324 entrants. It wasn't a bad start to my tournament season. I beat 75 percent of the players before busting out. But, I was still about 250 players short of the money, and there would be no Day 2 possibility unless I fired another bullet at the event the next afternoon. Just because I don't favor rebuy tournaments doesn't mean I won't play them, and I had allotted two bullets for Colossus, so I drove back to my rented condo unit, went online, and purchased a seat for another shot at fame, fortune and fulfillment of my poker dream.

Colossus: Strike Two
I should have known problems lay ahead when I was assigned a table in the Miranda room and nobody read me my rights. As it turned out they weren't needed, as I was the victim of a poker mugging, rather than the perpetrator. The term *card dead* was created for just my situation. As I sat through three orbits (twenty-four hands) with no hole cards totaling more than 18 combined, hands such as 7-2, 8-6, 4-2, 9-6, 5-7, 10-2, *ad infinitum*.

I only saw *paint* (jack, queen or king) six times during this drought, and each one was paired with a low companion (2-8).

When I finally did receive a decent hand, J-J, I raised $800, was put all in by another player with a stack six times my size, and I snap-called. Hey, I had the 4th best starting hand. I turned over my jacks. He turned over a K-10. I am a favorite to win.

The dealer and the cards don't get the message, as a king in the *window* (first visible card on the flop) ends my second attempt at a Colossus victory. I begin my walk of shame out of the room. Desperately seeking to salvage anything from this crushing defeat I begin to wonder if this modicum of exercise will translate into weight loss on my diet.

Colossus: Strike Three and I'm Out

My bust-out was painful and short. Unfortunately, it was so quick that the blinds were not that high. This meant that I could rebuy into the tournament and still have over sixteen big blinds worth of chips. Of course, I had already committed two bullets to the tournament, and I wasn't in the best frame of mind to re-enter. I was on tilt so bad I had to walk along the wall so I wouldn't fall over. OK, that is an exaggeration, but I was in a negative space, and that's not an optimal time to commit more funds to what will, most likely, be a losing cause.

Regardless, I rebuy anyway. This is probably further proof that my days as a problem gambler are not behind me. I grab my seat assignment and go to my table, only to find another player sitting in it. The dealer looks at my receipt and informs me that, as a late entry, I need to draw for a new seat at table 12.

I ask him where table 12 is.

"See that line over there?" he gestures. There is no problem spotting where table 12 is located.

It takes an additional five minutes to finally get a valid seat assignment. By now the tournament is halfway through Level 5. Each round will cost me $950, about 20 percent of my stack. Translation: I'm in no position to sit back and wait for a premium hand to try and stay alive in the tournament. It's time to gamble, baby!

Suddenly, just when I had almost forgotten the lost art of winning, I begin to pick up some decent hands and pots. I work my $5,000 stack up to just under $10,000. I'm feeling good. I start thinking of my summer goal of placing in the money in at least one tournament and wonder if I had set my sights too low. Who knows? A gold bracelet wasn't off the table. What a beautiful story that would make! Amazing what a small rush will do to one's confidence, particularly after being card dead for round after round.

My fall to Earth is quicker than Icarus experienced on his ill-fated attempt to visit the sun. It starts out with a bad beat. I go all in with a pair of sixes and am called by my namesake pocket deuces. I am a clear favorite to win until the dealer put up a straight on the board, ending my hopes of a double-up with a split pot.

Impatient to get what is "rightfully" my $10,000 back, I have trouble waiting to get back in action. Thus, eight hands later when I look down at a 10-J suited, I decide to make a $1,000 bet and take down the pot right there. I get one caller who has position on me. The flop comes K-7-4 rainbow, completely missing my hand. No problem. I decide this is an appropriate time to run a bluff. When a bluff works, it is a beautiful sight; when it doesn't, it is an intense, eyeball-scorching glimpse of hell. I bet $2,000 figuring the king is a good scare card. It isn't scary enough, and I get called. The turn is another king. Now, at this point, I should check and fold to any raise. But I am in full bluff mode and bet an additional $4,000, hoping my aggressive line will encourage a fold by my opponent. I get called again.

The river produces yet a third king, and I know my only chance to win the hand is to fire one more raise, which I do with all my remaining chips. I don't get an immediate call. That is a good thing. But my opponent doesn't muck his hand, either. That is a bad thing.

Instead he thinks for a while before finally saying, "I just have to see your quad kings," calling my bet, and turning over pocket queens.

Exit one Duckman from Colossus.

In retrospect, had only one king hit the board, my bluff would have probably worked, but my chances of holding the one remaining king with three on the board were slight, and my opponent took full advantage of that information to make the call.

One of the worst aspects of tournament play is when you bust out and realize you're no longer in action. The longer you play, and the more money you have invested, the worse this feeling becomes.

I walked out of the Rio in a kind of semi-daze, not really returning to reality until I got to my car, unlocked the door, and promptly burned my hands on the steering wheel, a standard summer hazard in Vegas when your automobile has been sitting in 100+ degree heat for several hours.

I retire to my room to allow myself a proper sulking period.

"There's always tomorrow," I remind myself. But even that isn't assured at my age.

Then I get an idea. Maybe I can hit the daily double of losing. I haven't weighed in for a week and a few pounds lost might help soften the blow of the tournament debacle. I take the elevator down to the fitness center and prepare to weigh-in. On May 16, the official starting day of my trip, I hit the scales at 209 with the goal of losing at least twenty-five pounds by the time I returned home. I step on the scale without my usual fanfare of taking anything off my body that could increase my weight and am rewarded with a beautiful sight. I've broken through the 200-pound barrier. The digital readout is clear, and I check it twice for reliability. The results are the same. I weigh 197.5 pounds. Eleven-and-a-half pounds in three weeks.

At least I'm losing pounds along with the dollars. That puts me in a much better mood, tempered somewhat by the realization that my next tournament appearance will present me with challenges I've never faced before.

Some Colossus Facts and Figures

(1) There were a total of 18,053 Colossus entries, half of which (9,074) came from players who registered to play more than once. One participant entered the Colossus *12 times* (the maximum number allowed)!

(2) Gender imbalance: male registrants outnumbered female registrants 17 to 1.

(3) The youngest player was 21, the oldest 93.

(4) Each player started with 5,000 in chips, and the eventual winner ended up with over 90 million!

(5) A total of 884 dealers were needed to keep the tournament running smoothly.

(6) The average age of entrants was 41 years, 8 months.

(7) Participants came from seventy-six different countries to compete in the event.

CHAPTER 5

It's Snowing in Vegas

**I have one major advantage by playing this game
for the first time in my life:
I won't make the same mistakes I've made in the past.**

A new day, a new tournament. A new chance for redemption. And, in this case, a chance to play a new game, as in I never played it before in my life new, the $1,500, 2-7 lowball draw tournament.

At this point, any sane person would wonder why I would take a shot at winning a tournament featuring a game with which I had no experience. Ahhh, there is method to my madness. It turns out this particular form of poker is not that well-known or commonly played, thus, it will probably draw the smallest number of entries, giving me a better shot at a bracelet than the hold'em tournaments with their huge pool of entrants. Further, 2-7 lowball rewards gamblers who have the worst poker hand, the type I seem to receive most frequently in regular hold'em. Thus, I figure I have an edge in the poor hand department, even though my rational mind tells me that poor vs. good hands in poker are randomly distributed among players.

Today, I choose to live the myth rather than love the math.

Even though I have never played a hand of 2-7 lowball doesn't mean I am entering the fray unprepared. I spent a day scouring the Internet for information concerning how the game is played and what the optimal strategy is for winning hands. As such, I now have a rudimentary understanding of how to, hopefully, build a healthy chip stack.

The game of 2-7 lowball is basically draw poker with the major difference being that the worst poker hand wins the pot. Each game involves blinds and, depending on the house rules, antes, which increase at regular intervals (levels). As indicated, the goal is to get the worst poker hand possible; which, in 2-7 lowball is 7-5-4-3-2 of different suits. An ace is only played high in this game, which is why 6-4-3-2-A is not the worst hand. Straights and flushes count against you in 2-7 lowball as well. The winner of any contested hand is the player who has the worst hand, based on ranks. For example, any 9-high hand beats a 10-high hand. But if two players have a 9-high hand, then the other cards come into play, and 9-7-5-3-2 wins over a 9-7-6-3-2. Five card lowball hands of 8- and 7-high are premium.

Each hand consists of two betting rounds. The first betting round begins after every player has been dealt five cards face down. After players have looked at their hands, betting proceeds around the table just as in hold'em. However, in hold'em, where you can simply stay in the hand by calling the big blind, in the WSOP 2-7 lowball rules, the first player to enter the pot must open with a raise (not a call). Once the round of betting is complete, the remaining players are then given the opportunity to discard any or all their cards and receive new ones. It is unusual to see a seasoned 2-7 lowball player request more than two cards. Usually, if any cards are replaced, one card is the norm. If any players opt to keep the original cards they were dealt, they *stand pat,* exchange no cards. After all players have had a chance to discard any unwanted cards from their hands and receive new ones, a final round of betting commences. If more than one player remains after the second betting round, a showdown occurs, with the worst poker hand winning the pot, a tie between the two hands results in a chopped pot.

There are some general strategy tips that can help guide your play and increase your chances of winning. For example, if you have a jack-high hand, and your opponent draws one card, you are a favorite to win if both players bet the hand to showdown. Position is also extremely important in this game—more so than in hold'em. Being able to see if your opponent stands pat or discards one or more cards is critical information to learn before you decide how to play your hand.

Finally, bluffing plays a huge role in this form of poker, so much so that it has its own name—*snowing.* Being from Minneapolis, I figure that gives me an edge in the game.

This tournament begins at 3:00 PM. Each player starts with $7,500 in chips and the first day of play is divided into ten one-hour levels, with blinds starting at $25/$50 and increasing each hour. During the first hour of play, the player on the button is required to ante $75. Once the second hour begins, all players are required to post antes, which, like the blinds, increase as the levels progress.

*****

It's 2:30 now, and I'm getting all my supplies together before heading to the Rio. This includes two protein bars, my table assignment, my chip protector, car keys, safe deposit key, driver's license, total rewards card, reading glasses, extra money, tape recorder, phone, duck-caller (don't ask), room key, and a jacket to store all my stuff

It's almost time to shuffle up and deal!

I arrive at the Rio in plenty of time to print out my seating permit and find my assigned table. The tournament starts on time and I settle in for, hopefully, a long and fruitful day of poker.

During the first hour of action, I take note of my opponents play. It is said that if you can't identify the sucker at your table within that time frame, then that sucker is you! Frankly, I think the whole notion of reading the table in such a short period of time is highly exaggerated. If it were true, more players would be doing it. At most of the poker tables I frequent, at least half of the participants are on their cell phones, playing games on their iPads, or watching sporting events that play out on super-sized TV monitors throughout the room.

Plus, many players are hard to read, either because they are constantly mixing up the way they play or they don't follow any set way of playing. That is one reason why amateur players are such a challenge for professionals. They don't play according to the "book" and lack the knowledge to be influenced by expert moves set into motion to deceive them.

> **TIPS AND QUIPS: QUIP #4**
> A player once told me he couldn't get a read on me and didn't know what I was going to do. I told him I didn't know what I was going to do, either. And I was telling the truth.

It doesn't take me long to realize that my tablemates are not following the advice I learned on the Internet. Several times I see players make opening bets and then request two cards when given the chance to stand pat or exercise their discard option.

As the hours pass, I notice that 8-high hands usually win, whereas 10-high hands seem to be less successful in taking down pots. It doesn't take me long to realize that getting five cards where none of them is over 10, all are different (no pairs), and there are no straights or flushes, is a relatively rare occurrence.

Also, I note that some higher alien life form has interceded in our game with the sole purpose of taunting me.

Why? Because I suddenly start picking up five cards that contain fantastic hold'em hands—three of a kind, two pair, once even quads! Of course, in lowball, these are exactly the hands you don't want to see.

After four hours of play I am basically on life support. My tiny stack of $7,500 chips has shrunk to $2,300, and I know that, if I don't double up soon, I will be faced with elimination and the dreaded dilemma of whether I should or should not rebuy myself back into the tournament.

I hold on, winning a few small pots to keep my stack size steady. But as time passes, I'm falling further behind the average stack size for all players, which turns out to be 266 entrants, each paying $1,500 to try and capture the first-place prize money of $89,000 and change, plus the gold bracelet.

By hour nine, I am down to my lowest chip level of the day, $2,200. Then, it happens. Bam! Bam! Bam! Bam! I double up four times in a row and find myself sitting on a stack of $30,000+ chips. I ride that momentum to the end of Day 1, bagging $39,000 in chips and sitting in 18th place with 50 players remaining.

I return to my rented condominium to plot my Day 2 strategy. Based on my BMW approach, I have achieved Step 1, bag, and now need to focus on Step 2, getting in the money. I make a pledge to play tight and focus on playing only premium hands until the bubble breaks and I'm in the top forty players who will cash.

So, what happens?

On the very first hand of the second day a small-stacked player goes all in as I look down at the best hand I had been dealt, a 7-6. If I call, I'll be risking over half of my stack. If I don't call, I don't think I'll ever be able to forgive myself. I call. The guy flips over a 9-6 and I take down the pot. That is the turning point for me. I basically coast until we get in the money, a lengthy effort, as the bubble actually lasts forty minutes.

During the break after the money bubble bursts I have the opportunity to meet Billy Baxter, "Mr. Lowball," who had already won four WSOP bracelets in this event. He also won an important tax case that established poker as a viable business, a legal battle that went all the way to the Supreme Court before it was resolved in Billy's favor. All professional poker players owe Billy Baxter a huge "thank you" for his tenacity in fighting and winning his tax case. It gives gamblers who play poker for a living and can show winnings the opportunity to take deductions, and take advantage of other tax breaks afforded businesses that were not available to gamblers prior to the Baxter Supreme Court ruling.

Returning to the tables I discover a new player has been moved to the three seat, Phil Hellmuth, who promptly gets in a verbal sparring match with another player to my left. I just sit and smile. Having gotten to know Phil personally while writing two books with him, I realize he is a great guy away from the table, and turns into "Poker-brat" as part of his poker persona. Meanwhile, I begin to hemorrhage chips, and it doesn't take long to realize that I have more important things to do than be entertained by table talk. My tournament life is ebbing away and I need to make a move.

My move came five hours and thirty minutes into Day 2. It was my last move of the tournament. I went all in on a natural 10-8. I didn't draw any cards and promptly lost to an 8-7. And, just like that, my lowball was a no-go-ball, and I was out in 17th place.

I couldn't believe it! In only my second WSOP event, I made the money, thus achieving one of my three major goals for the trip. I now had a WSOP cash under my belt and was feeling pretty smug.

Looking at the win from a financial point of view, however, presented me with a more somber perspective on my achievement. I had just completed playing fifteen-and-a-half hours of poker over two days, beating 249 of 266 players and been paid $3,572. After deducting my buy-in of $1,500 that left an actual win of $2,072, an hourly wage of $134 (before expenses). Not bad, but certainly not enough to become a full-time professional, at least not until I could cash in tournaments on a regular basis.

CHAPTER 6

◆━━━━━━◆

Can a Mere Mortal Capture the Giant?

*If you believe that poker is a game of luck,
then you will most likely go broke playing it.*

This bracelet event, the Giant, which is new to the WSOP lineup, is another weekend affair featuring multiple starting days spread over five Fridays, a low entry fee of $365, and unlimited re-entries. The Giant is designed to attract thousands of participants who can afford to play smaller buy-ins and enjoy the idea of turning a minimum investment into a million-dollar payday. Of course, the challenge of getting through a field of 18,000 like-minded competitors doesn't seem to deter them from their dream. Nor does it stop me, although my aspirations are much lower. As always, my major goal is to make the money. A deep run and even a final table is a distant goal on a horizon far away, not a priority.

As I ready myself for play in this, my third WSOP event, I think of my cash in the Goliath tournament at Planet Hollywood and hope that this Giant will prove as beneficial to my bankroll. Sadly, such is not the case. It was more like this Giant was the Biblical Goliath and I, David, minus the slingshot. I won't go into lengthy efforts to describe the bloody outcome. In fact, my participation in the Giant is basically the story of two poker hands.

The first hand unfolds early in the tournament. Starting with $20,000 in chips and facing 20-minute blinds, it is clear that big action would soon be the order of the day. At my table, the first blind level is relatively quiet, but with the second level, chips begin going to the middle like Canadians flocking to a hockey game. It is during this round that my first big hand plays out. I am in the big blind and peeking down at a 3♣ and 5♣. Three players call before my turn to act, leaving me the option of checking or raising. I check, deciding not to put additional money in the pot.

The flop comes out A-2-4 rainbow, with one club. I have just flopped a straight! An opponent in middle position raises to $1,300 and I call. Everyone else folds.

The turn brings a 7♣, giving me a possible flush draw as well. I raise $2,000, and my opponent reraises to $4,100. I consider this for a moment and three-bet to $10,000, bringing a snap all-in call from my opponent. I call with my few remaining chips. We turn over our cards. My opponent proudly flips over two fours for a set but quickly reassesses his mood when I reveal my boss straight. The river jack is of no help to either of us, and I basically double up.

Fast forward to Level 6. At this point, the blinds are $300/$600 with a $75 ante. It is also the last level before the first 20-minute bathroom break. With just two minutes to go in the level, I get my second critical hand. In the cutoff position, I look down at a pair of black eights and make a min-raise of $1,200. I get two callers. The flop comes 9-9-4 with two clubs. Everyone checks around. The turn is the 10♣, giving me a shot at a backdoor flush along with my pair of eights. One guy bets $2,000, and another calls, as do I. The river brings the 3♣, completing a small flush for me. One of the original $2,000 bettors now shoves all in, leaving me with a decision that will determine my tournament life. Because my all-in opponent has more chips than I do, should I call and lose, I'll be felted, lose all my chips and knocked out of the tournament. On the other hand, if I call and win, I will be in great shape to finish Day 1 in good chip position.

TIPS AND QUIPS: TIP #3

Anytime there is a break between sessions, it is critical that you tighten up your calling/betting range on the last hand before the break begins. This is because many players, particularly short-stacked ones, don't want to waste their time in a break only to return to a situation where they are likely to bust before making the money. Thus, they will often go all in on the pre-break hand in an effort to double-up and make the waiting around during break worthwhile. A good player with a premium hand can take advantage of this behavior because they will often be facing weaker than normal hands for the money wagered. What you don't want to do is be an early raiser in a pre-break hand before you have knowledge of what the other players intend to do. This is because of the higher likelihood that you will be called or raised by the "double-me-up" or "knock-me-out" short-stacked opponents yet to act.

In general, the longer the break, the higher the probability that marginally stacked players will bet aggressively. Thus, the break before dinner and the last hand on any day of a multi-day tournament is prime time for short stack betting.

A final point: If you are playing in a rebuy/re-enter tournament, be extremely cautious on the final few hands before the rebuy/re-enter period ends. Many players with short stacks will try and double-up or commit to fire a second bullet at this point. I have seen many players go all in on any two cards, hoping to double-up or buy back in. Players with premium hands can take advantage of this double-up or rebuy mentality by facing weaker holdings; but beware—suck-out possibilities are more likely when an opponent is willing to play any two cards!

I call the all in and the third player folds. As I get ready to turn over my hand at showdown I'm hoping that my opponent has trip nines and not a higher flush. Well, I get my wish, but not exactly the way I had envisioned it. My opponent did have three nines; in fact, he had *four* nines, giving him quads and sending me to the parking lot.

Talk about a dramatic turn-around in the game and a classic demonstration of how a chip leader can become a chip bleeder on the turn of a card!

My only consolation to the day's event was losing to four of a kind rather than some wimpy three-outer on the river. My opponent had a better hand from the get-go and deserved to win. That he did so in such spectacular fashion was a stark reminder that even very good hands, like my flush, are not locks when played all the way to the river.

My next crack at climbing the Giant's "chipstalk" would be next Friday. I had fallen once, but I wasn't down for the count. I reminded myself of the oft-quoted statement,

"It's not how many times you fall that matters, it's how many times you fall and get back up."

I would be standing and ready for Round 2 of the Giant in a week.

CHAPTER 7

Who Wants to Be a Millionaire?

Poker is better than sex because you can do it more often, and it lasts longer.

The Millionaire Maker tournament is, as its name suggests, a bracelet event that guarantees the winner a minimum of $1 million. The previous year's winner bagged $1,065,403. To generate that kind of prize pool at only $1,500 a pop requires lots of entries; thus, there are two flights, a Day 1 on Saturday and another on Sunday, with one re-entry allowed per flight. Thus, a player can enter the tournament four times if he or she had the $6,000 and an overabundance of optimism. (Even baseball players understand that after three strikes, you're out.)

I only entered once, that's the good news. The bad news is the amount of action I got for my investment—four hands of poker!

With a starting stack of $7,500, 60-minute levels, and blinds starting at $25/$50, this is a better structure than most of the WSOP events for giving the player some time to maneuver and actually wait for premium starting hands before getting pot involved. It doesn't have that shove fest aspect that many of the low-starting stack, short level bracelet events serve up.

So, what do I do? I get it all in during the first round of play, tabling 10-10 against A-K for a quick double-up or tournament elimination. Do not ask me why I did this. Maybe I picked up a tell, maybe I just was too excited to see a premium pair so early in the tournament, maybe I just wanted to gamble it up. After all, I have been known to be a degenerate gambler in, hopefully, the past.

In retrospect, the bet wasn't a bad one, considering I got it in good being I was a slight favorite to win, about 53/47 percent. The problem was I was risking all my chips on what was basically a coin flip when, if I had wanted to commit all my chips, I had plenty of time to wait for a far better holding to make such a move.

Of course, the flop produced the dreaded ace, and I was homeward bound less than ten minutes after I sat down to play. This, of course, is one of the most difficult aspects of tournament poker, knowing how long you'll be playing on any given day. It's also one of the saddest, particularly when you make dinner plans with another tournament player, and you don't even make it past lunch.

I went home and sulked. I tried to keep reminding myself that the very nature of tournament poker is the fact that even the best players only place in the money about 20 percent of the time. I had already accomplished that feat by winning money in one of my first four tournaments.

The realization that I was winning at a 25 percent clip should have cheered me. It didn't. My problem was I hated to lose. And, in poker, losing is something you have to learn to live with. I had a lot to learn!

TIPS AND QUIPS: QUIP #5

I suggested to my wife that I play poker for a living. She said I wouldn't last long.

I thought she was talking about my bankroll.

CHAPTER 8

●◆ ——————— ◆●

Las Vegas on $20,000 a Day

**I got comped on my room
and paid for the hotel.**

When I first got my idea to take the summer off and play the WSOP, I decided to budget for one high buy-in tournament, the $10,000 main event. Now, I will reveal to you how a recovering, but not fully recovered, degenerate gambler thinks.

Degenerate me: "I see that there's another no limit 2-7 lowball championship tournament on tap for tomorrow. The entry fee is $10,000, which means less entrants and more chance to win a bracelet. Besides, I placed in the money the last 2-7 tournament I was in."

Recovering-degenerate me: "Whoa! You're still on tilt from losing your last tournament in four hands. Don't do anything impulsive you'll live to regret. The best lowball players in the world will be in that $10,000 event, a much tougher field than you faced in the smaller $1,500 buy-in tourney."

Degenerate me: "The best predictor of future performance is past performance. I can do this. I've won before, why shouldn't I succeed again?"

Recovering-degenerate me: $10,000 to test out your theory is out of line. And you're getting out of control. Save your money and divide it up so you can play in smaller priced tournaments."

Degenerate me: "Higher rewards require greater risks. This might be my only chance to play in this tournament. If I don't do it, I'll always be left wondering what might have been had I been willing to play."

Recovering-degenerate me: "And you're seriously ready to risk 20 percent of your bankroll to find out?"

Degenerate me: "I'm already purchasing my ticket online as we speak."

****

Which is how I find myself at the Rio at 3:00 PM on a Sunday afternoon ready to do battle with some of the most fear-inspiring poker players on the face of the planet. The fact that I recognize some of the faces around me is evidence enough that I am the high school varsity basketball senior who has accidently been assigned to play a game in the NBA.

I sit quietly in my seat, counting my starting stack of $50,000 chips and trying to look like a man who should be playing in the world championship of a game he has played but once before. I don't think my tablemates are buying it, but, as good fortune would have it, on the first round of cards, I call a raise, draw one card, and end up winning $12,000 chips when I hit the second best possible hand (a 7-6-5-3-2). It will be the best hand I have for the rest of the tournament, but, of course, at the time I don't know that. The win boosts my confidence.

Sadly, confidence and competence are not the same thing, as my gradual chip erosion clearly reveals. It isn't like I am getting hammered by my opponents, rather I am losing pots by the tiniest of margins: 10-9 vs. 10-8, 9-8 vs. 9-6. But a loss, nonetheless. Even with the generous stack of starting chips and the lengthy blinds (60 minutes) I find myself down to the point that even an all-in bet would hardly generate much fold equity. So, of course, I go all in with a 9-8 and lose to a 9-6.

$10,000 down the proverbial poker drain in less than three hours! Could things get any worse?

Of course.

You see, this particular event allowed one re-entry, and I hadn't used mine—yet.

Thus, the brief and heated conversation between me and myself, Part II.

Degenerate me: "I got knocked out so fast the blinds are low enough for me to rebuy."

Recovering-degenerate me: "Are you *serious?* You just got trounced and lost $10,000 in the process. Now you want to spend another $10,000 to get whipped again? That's 40 percent of your bankroll in one day, in one tournament, in one contest you have no chance of winning based on what just happened over the past three hours."

Degenerate me: (Moving quickly out of the tournament room and walking swiftly to the rebuy window down the hall.) "The second time's the charm. A little luck at the right time, plus a bit more patience on my end and I know I can get in the money. Hey, there's only 100 entries, that's a 1 in a 100 shot at a gold bracelet. I'll never get odds that good again."

Recovering-degenerate me: "You're out of control."

Degenerate me: (Reaching rebuy window.) "I want to re-enter the 2-7 lowball event. Let me in my safe deposit box, and I'll get you the money. Here's the key."

Ten minutes later I find myself seated at a different table with a nice, new stack of $50,000 chips. I feel cocky. I feel giddy. I feel that Lady Luck is wrapping herself around my body.

Sure enough, on the first hand I am dealt, I raise $14,000 in chips, get one caller, and promptly win the pot with a 9 low. Things are looking up. I'm confident that it won't be long before I see my self-named "Happy Squirrel," a 7-5-4-3-2, the absolute nuts. What squirrel wouldn't be happy with those tasty morsels?

The Happy Squirrel never pays me a visit. The closest I get to the nuts is the bag of cashews in my jacket pocket. My second effort to cash the 2-7 championship event is turning out to be disturbingly a carbon copy of my first attempt. My chip stack is melting faster than a block of ice in the Vegas heat.

Could this really be happening?

The answer is a despondent "yes," as I crash and burn for a second time, not even close to bagging any chips.

As my last chips disappear across the green felt (my 10-8 loses to a 10-6) I stagger out of my chair and head for the hallway and hoped-for obscurity. The dealer's call of "seat open" reaches my ears before I clear the door.

****

Back in the privacy of my room I sit in my chair and stare out the window at the cloudless Vegas sky. On the table in front of me is an old copy of *Gambling Times* magazine I brought with me. The publication is twenty-five years old. I turn to a column I wrote that month, a book review of Anthony Holden's *Big Deal*, the story of how the English writer and critic had taken a year off from his job to play poker on a $20,000 budget. The subtitle of my column was, "Poker on $20,000 a year." I gave the book a glowing review, my closing observation recommending "... Mr. Holden's book for any reader who wants to learn more about poker and/or wants to vicariously enjoy a trip of a lifetime. In the world of gambling, this book is truly a 'Big Deal,' and a good one."

I think that's when it hit me. I had spent in one day what Anthony Holden had budgeted for an entire year. Well, one could rationalize that $20,000 in 1991 was a lot more than $20,000 in 2017, but the fact remained: I had lost control of myself and knocked out almost half my gambling budget in less than six hours.

I got back in my car and drove directly to the Rio. I went to my safety deposit box, retrieved $10,000 of the original $50,000 that once was there and immediately purchased my ticket for the WSOP main event. I wanted to be sure—no matter how crazy I got—that I would still be funded to play the main event.

I felt terrible about the events of the day. But I still had money left, which meant I wasn't out of action. There would be another tournament tomorrow, another chance to win money. And, of course, there was always the chance of making a final table and winning hundreds of thousands of dollars. I had to remember that my Vegas poker adventure wasn't meant to be a 100-yard-dash but, rather, a six-week marathon; which, it turned out, was very appropriate, considering that the next day's event was called the Marathon.

TIPS AND QUIPS: TIP #4

It turns out that there are a lot of excellent writers who have published books on how they took time off from the regular jobs to embark on a poker journey. Three books, like this one, tell of the author's adventures as they take time off to do battle across the green felt. I highly recommend them for your reading pleasure and enhancement of your poker knowledge.

(1) James McManus, *Positively Fifth Street*. James goes to Vegas to cover the Binion murder trial and ends up playing—and final-tabling—the main event.

(2) Anthony Holden, *Big Deal: One Year as a Professional Poker Player*. A stimulating, eye-opening journey into poker venues around the world. A follow-up book is also a reading delight: Anthony Holden, *Bigger Deal: A Year on the New Poker Circuit*.

---

(3) Al Alvarez, *The Biggest Game in Town*. Another excellent writer details his experiences in the world of high-stakes poker.

CHAPTER 9

Entered the "Marathon"
Ran for a Mile

The most likely candidate to
beat you at the table is yourself.

It is the morning of my 29th day in Vegas. I get out of bed, pull back the curtains and marvel at the cloudless sky that has greeted me every day since my arrival. The brightness of the day brings a degree of joy to a man who braved the dreary, cloudy days of his youth in Minnesota. It also illuminates my memories of yesterday's financial meltdown.

It's hard to feel excited and optimistic about playing in another poker tournament less than twenty-four hours after suffering two devastating losses in the lowball championship, but play I must. It goes against my rule about playing in the right mindset, yet my book assignment overrides this consideration. I suck it up and head out into the 105-degree morning.

Over at the Rio, I walk to my table, trying to maintain my confident poker posture. After showing the dealer my ID and buy-in ticket, he pushes me a stack of $26,200 chips. The odd number of chips has to do with the length of a marathon, which, hopefully, will find me as a front-runner as the race develops. I note that each playing level is 100 minutes long, which, along with the number of starting chips and slowly escalating blind structure is ideal for discouraging shove fests. The tournament is also a freezeout, which means that players can't make high-risk bets in an attempt to double up and then re-enter if they are unsuccessful. In the Marathon, when you're out of chips, you're out of the race—for good.

There are still several seats open as I look around the table at my opposition, the usual collection of hoodies with their cell phones, sunglasses and ear phones, middle-aged men dressed like they had the week off or were already retired, and the mandatory female, in this case a 20-something gal with curly hair and a WSOP sweatshirt covering her ample breasts. Yes, male poker players do notice these things.

Five minutes before the event is scheduled to start, management pipes in music from Clint Eastwood's film, *The Good, The Bad, and the Ugly.* This happens before every event. I wonder if this is the WSOP's subtle reminder to each player to assess the adjective that best suits his or her play. I'm stuck on *ugly*, still smarting over my double-defeat less than a day earlier.

"Shuffle up and deal!"

The traditional announcement to begin play gives me the tingle of anticipation that always precedes the start of an event and shifts my mind into focus mode. My first two cards come spinning over and I get my first hand of the day. I look at the first card, a 7, and the second, a deuce, a 7-2, the worst starting hand in the game. When my turn to act arrives, I toss my cards into the muck, wondering if the 7-2 is a harbinger of things to come.

Sadly, yes. From the get-go, I am card dead. Hand after hand cards come with no paint (J, Q, K), no ace, not even a small pair. My marathon performance is mimicking a weekend jogger rather than a long-distance runner.

It's at times like this when, I truly believe, all poker players question why they are participating in such an infernal ritual. I remind myself of *variance*, the poker player's excuse for long periods of winless play. I think of the mathematical concept of *random walk*, where the normal course of events are dramatically altered, for example, fifteen straight reds at roulette; five nines in a row at the crap table, and assure myself that things will even out and I will once again receive my fair share of good cards.

Well, it turns out that the Marathon is just one gargantuan random walk for yours truly. When I finally do see a good hand, K-K, I cannot contain myself and shove my chips into a pot that has already been raised by one player and called by two others. The two callers drop out, but the original raiser calls my all in. To make matters worse, he has me covered.

We turn over our cards, and I get about the best outcome I could hope for. My opponent shows down A-K unsuited, so, basically, he's got three outs—the other three aces—to beat me. On the other hand, if my superior starting hand holds up and I double through my opponent, I will have more chips than my original stack, the first time that would have occurred in this tournament.

So, what happens?

As the dealer spreads the flop, there is the A♦ in the window. The old *ace magnet* (pocket kings are believed to attract aces on the flop, turn, or river) works its wonder and knocks me out of the tournament.

Do I believe in something as mathematically ridiculous as an ace magnet effect?

You bet your life I do! In all honesty, I must admit that poker players have developed fantastic selective memories, they will remember for a lifetime when a flopped ace beats their pocket kings, but forget the other ten times no ace appeared at all. At any rate, I am down another $2,620 and take my leave into the 110-degree heat of the Rio parking lot, where my blisteringly hot car patiently awaits my arrival. After burning my hand on the door handle and steering wheel, I manage to drive back to my condo unit, where I curl up in a fetal position and drift off into a restless slumber.

CHAPTER 10

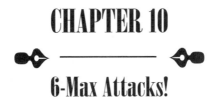

6-Max Attacks!

If you can't find any jokers in the deck,
they might be sitting next to you.

OK, it's "try a new strategy" time. Nearly comatose from my string of tournament losses, I decide that, if I can't win at a ten-player table, perhaps I'll fare better at a game where only five players are opposing me. Buoyed by this hope, I sign up to play in the $3,000, 6-handed no-limit tournament, which has $15,000 in starting chips, 60-minute levels, and blinds starting at $25/$50.

I figure this structure should give me plenty of time to pick my spots, but I fail to take into account the fact that the blinds will be coming around with greater frequency due to the reduced number of contestants at the table. Nevertheless, I'm feeling a moderate level of confidence: rather remarkable considering the recent string of losses I have endured.

As I'm waiting for the tournament to begin, I note that last year's winner of this event won over half-a-million dollars and over $22 million in prize money was paid out to winning players. I figure it's time for me to take down a hunk of cash, and I start thinking about what luxury car I want to purchase for the ride back to Tampa.

The tournament begins and it seems that the gold bracelet has my name on it. In the early going, I get two incredible suck outs, once when my pocket queens beat my opponent's pocket aces thanks to a queen on the river, and again when I go up against an A-Q with an A-6 and hit a magical three-outer 6 on the turn. My stack is a beautiful sight to behold. I peer over my chips, like a general over his troops, and get ready to send them back into battle.

For a while, I'm table captain, steadily adding to my chip stack, stealing blinds, and winning the few hands that go to showdown.

Then, things turn. And, in poker, when you start losing hands, things can go south in a heartbeat. It's almost as if my opposition can feel my cloak of invincibility has been ripped from my body, and wagers I make—that would previously have gone uncontested—are now called, even raised. My good hands, which previously would have stood up against slightly inferior ones, are now being edged out by opponents revealing marginally better holdings.

The hand that ultimately did the most damage to my tournament life and sent me into a fatal tailspin was my A-K against an opponent's Q-Q. With a huge pot in the middle of the table, the hand ran out J-5-7-5-9, while I nearly ran out of chips. The carnage was completed a few hands later when I shoved my remaining stack with pocket nines on an 8-high board (8-4-6-2-3) and was called by a guy holding pocket tens.

Once again, I was forced to get up from my chair and perform the walk of shame to the nearest exit, which, mercifully, was only a few feet away. Today would go down as just another loss in my six-week tournament battle, the details of which would soon be forgotten as my poker struggles continued.

Strangely, the one memory that will always stay with me from this tournament didn't involve the hands I played, my opponents, or even my pulverizing loss but, rather, our dealer, Kim. She was a short woman with short arms and, to pull in the chips that were beyond her reach, she used a little blue rake to get them to the center of the table. It was the first time I had actually seen the casino "rake"! I might have appreciated the humor in the situation if it wasn't for the fact that Kim was raking in my chips until the green felt in front of me looked like my lawn back in Minneapolis when the trees were bare and all the leaves on the lawn had been swept away.

All I knew for sure was that I needed to turn over a new leaf and start winning if my WSOP dream summer was not going to evolve into a winter of discontent.

CHAPTER 11

Can I Surpass My WSOP Summer Objective?

Ba-a, ba-a black sheep, are you full of bull?
No sir, no sir—aces full!
One for my fortune, one for my fame
and one to get paid in this torrid poker game.

After five straight losses and a bankroll depletion of 50 percent I am starting to channel the Tampa Bay Buccaneers during their early years in Tampa. The good news: I may have lost five straight times, but they lost twenty-six! The bad news: if they could lose twenty-six straight games, what's to stop me from continuing my losing streak?

These thoughts are spinning through my head as I prepare to compete in my 8th WSOP event, a $2,500, 3-day tournament with $12,500 in starting chips and 60-minute levels.

The first two levels are almost placid, as no one seems anxious to put in any large bets. One big blind actually gets a *walk*, wins the blinds without opposition, in the second level, the only time I have ever seen that happen so early in a tournament when the blinds are so small. By the beginning of the fourth level, play begins to open up a bit, but I am still stuck within $200 of, my starting stack.

Then, along comes the defining hand of the tournament for me. I look down and see a pair of fives in the small blind in an unraised pot and make it $4,000 to go. I figured it was an easy way to pick up the blinds and antes, and, even if the big blind called, I still had a decent hand.

So, what does the big blind do? He goes all in! I tank for a while and decide that he probably has A-x, meaning he'll have to outdraw my fives to win. Of course, I could be wrong, he could already have a higher pair, which would make me a 5-1 underdog and likely send me packing.

I decide to call. The best I can hope for is a coin flip, so it is not a good move (probably why I am currently on a losing streak). Sometimes your gut screams "bet," and that's what you do.

We turn our hands face up, and I discover my read was good. My opponent holds A-J, two overcards, to my pair. The flop comes rag-rag-J, making me a huge favorite to be on a six-tournament losing streak. The turn brings a queen, not changing anything. And then, on the river, that lovely flowing body of water, floats a 5♣, giving me a set and, most important, doubling the chips I had less than a minute earlier. I have life, I have chips, I have hope, I have not wet my pants. All is good in the world of poker and I hear the siren call of good fortune.

I can feel myself exuding confidence as the levels pass and the blinds and antes increase. I am winning enough hands to keep me well above the average chip stack in the room and am closing in on the "B" of my BMW poker goal: I am in a position to bag chips for Day 2.

During Level 8, the final level of play for Day 1, I look down at my hole cards and see my first pocket aces in two tournaments. The guy to my right makes a min-raise to $1,200. I smooth call. The flop appears to be unremarkable: 3-7-9 rainbow. I bet $2,000, and my opponent calls. The turn brings a 10♥. With the board straightening, I bet $4,000 and get an all in response from my lone competitor, which I snap call. We flip over our cards, and I see I am playing my two aces against J-J. A little 5 on the river doesn't affect the outcome. I take down a really nice pot just as we are getting ready to bag, which, ten minutes later, I do.

Now I am through to Day 2 and step two of my BMW—get in the money.

Day 2 begins where Day 1 left off, this time with a Duckman flourish. Because I am known to play deuces strongly—I even wear a shirt with two deuces on them—I often gets calls on my before-the-flop raises because my opponents put me on deuces and they have a better hand. On the third hand of Day 2, I get pocket deuces and make a ridiculously high 10x-the-big-blind bet of $4,000. Usually, such a huge bet discourages further bets, and I take down the pot uncontested.

But, in this case, a short-stacked player goes all in, leaving me with the choice of folding, and losing my $4,000 bet, or calling and possibly losing $11,000 to what is, most likely, already a better hand than I hold.

"Honor the deuces!" I call out of respect to my "do the deuces" reputation.

Sure enough, my opponent turns over pocket queens against my lowly deuces. The flop and the turn bring no significant cards, and I am already trying to figure out how badly $11,000 is going to decimate my stack when the river brings…another deuce! I remember saying to myself, quietly enough so my opponent wouldn't hear it:

> **TIPS AND QUIPS: QUIP #6**
> **A duck on the end**
> **is the Duckman's best friend!**

Hours of play pass. I stay well ahead of the average chip count and try to win at least one hand an orbit. We reach the bubble, and I vow to bet nothing but pocket aces, determined to make the money. When the bubble finally breaks, I am still well-stacked and have now surpassed my original goal of cashing in at least one WSOP tournament. I am a two-time winner!

Can it get much better than this?

Unfortunately, no. At least, not in this tournament. In a turning point hand not long after the bubble bursts, I get it all in with two other players. One guy has about $60,000, I have slightly more. The problem is the third all in has the biggest stack at the table and has us both covered. The winner of this hand will be well up there on the chip leaderboard.

We flip over our hands. I show 10-10; my opponents have, respectively, A-6 suited and A-J suited. I've got to fade a lot of cards to win, but with two aces already showing, I like my chances. The flop comes 6-Q-4 with two hearts. My A-J opponent has hearts, so I have to dodge any ace, jack or heart to win a monster pot. The turn brings paint and it's red. Luckily it is neither a jack or a heart but a K♦. Now all I have to do is dodge the A-J and heart for one more card. And the final card is the 8♥, giving my opponent the nut flush, the pot and my chance to win the tournament.

I finish up 48th out of 1,086 for a payout of $4,344 which, minus my buy-in of $2,500 means a win of $1,844. Certainly not a large bite out of the $20,000 I lost on the two $10,000 lowball entries from a few days earlier—but a step in the right direction. Plus, I was a winner!

Now, can I make it two wins in a row?

CHAPTER 12

Will You Still Bet Me, Will You Still Sweat Me, When I'm 65?

During a super senior's tournament, it was the small blind's turn to act. Suddenly the big blind fell from his chair; dead of a massive heart attack. Seeing the man next to him die so distressed the small blind that he, too, suffered a life-ending coronary. The dealer called the floor for a ruling, and it was determined that the big blind acted out of turn.

When I was a teenager, kids my age used to believe that people over sixty were ancient. Yet, I now find myself playing alongside individuals who are all sixty-five or older, and I wonder, "Where did the years go?" The fact that I'm ten years older than the minimum entry age and still feel alive makes me realize that age is a number that doesn't always reflect the physical or mental agility of the individual in question.

As play commences, it becomes evident that the years have not dulled the skills of my tablemates to any significant degree; in fact, what brain cells might have been lost are more than made up for by experience and well-honed instincts.

In other words, winning the Super Seniors Tournament is not going to be the cakewalk I had suspected. Ironically, it turns out that my age does play a role in my performance, but not due to mental deterioration but, rather, due to failing eyesight. During the first few minutes of the second blind level, I peer down at my hole cards and see a beautiful A♣-10♣. Because of the tournament structure—and a small starting stack of only $5,000—there isn't much room for error or waiting for the absolute nuts to make a move. I raise $500 and get two callers. We all see the 3-8-Q flop, with two of the cards being clubs. I check, the next player to act bets $1,000, and the third player folds.

When it comes back around to me I call. The turn produces a beautiful, smiling lady, the Q♣. I have the nut flush.

My opponent calls "all in," and I literally beat him into the pot with an instacall. As we await the river, we show our hands. My opponent has A-Q, giving him top set, top kicker, normally a monster hand. I know he's going to be hurting badly when he sees my boss flush, and I quickly turn over my cards so as not to be accused of a slow roll.

I watch my opponent as he looks at my hand. He smiles and says, "I put you on a flush draw."

Before I can say anything else, the dealer burns and turns the river, a 3♦.

My opponent lets out his breath and says, "It's never easy," and pushes his stack toward the dealer for a count. We are very close in chips, but I think I have him covered. This could be a much-needed double-up for me.

Then, the dealer asks me to cut out $4,200 from my stack. I begin to ask him "What for?" when I take another look at my tabled hand. That's when I see it. My 10 is not a club, it's a spade! I don't have the nut flush, I have a four-flush, ace-high hand, hardly a threat against trip queens.

No wonder my opponent had been so happy when he saw my hand. I was a big dog with one card to come.

My visual mistake left me with less than $500 in chips, which I lost two hands later. Just like that, I was no longer a "super senior" but simply a "losing senior."

But wait! The WSOP, with its ever-changing rules, had decided to allow one re-entry into the tournament. An extra $1,000 to vindicate myself. Was it worth it? With my hatred of rebuy options, should I really exercise it? I literally ran to the rebuy window to get back in action before the blinds increased any further. I was damn sure not going to let those young seniors beat me out. Perhaps I should have thought things through a bit longer before I invested another $1,000 from my bankroll. Maybe Quip #7, below, was an accurate self-description.

> **TIPS AND QUIPS: Quip #7**
> If you get married and then divorced, what makes you think you'll do better the second time around?

No matter, within fifteen minutes, I was back in action with a new stack of $5,000 in chips and blinds at $75/$150.

I wish I could report that my second foray into the Land of the Aged ended happily. I wish I could have run over my table like a Hummer over a Honda. Sadly, I didn't even have time to dream of victory before my untimely demise well before the dinner break. I only played one hand in my second shot at being a Super Senior Success. My hand: pocket nines. My opponent: pocket sevens. Me: "All in." My opponent: "Call."

If you guessed that the guy sucked out on me by getting a third 7 on the river, you'd be wrong.

He got it on the turn.

It was time for my second walk of shame in one afternoon. I got out of my chair as gracefully as I could. If I couldn't beat older players, at least I could try and look like some younger Internet whiz that just walked into the wrong room. As I reached the door and bee-lined it to the sweltering parking lot I decided what I wanted engraved on my tombstone:

TIPS AND QUIPS: Quip # 8
I was all in when I went all out.

CHAPTER 13

A Father's Day Massacre

The only thing that makes less sense than playing weak hands out of position is eating hot dogs at a greyhound racing facility.

$5,000. That's what it's going to cost me to play my next event, a four-day, no-limit 6-handed tournament sporting 60-minute levels and $25,000 in starting chips. My bankroll is getting ever-lower. If my car ran on money, I'd be thinking about a fuel stop in my near future.

I wonder, should I skip this tournament and lower my potential losses? No! I made a pledge to play the series, and I'm not going to let a few—well, a lot—of defeats detour me from my goal.

When I arrive at my designated seat I get a shock. For some yet to be discovered reason, a camera crew is surrounding the table, obviously preparing to televise the proceedings. Why? I ask the player next to me, and he says something about a French pro sitting across from us. "I think they're doing a documentary on him," my tablemate comments. I look at the French player and think I recognize him. I can't be certain he's the cause of all of the attention. What I do know is that I am about to be part of a televised main table, adding a bit more pressure to my already fragile confidence.

If I couldn't beat a bunch of seniors, was I capable of holding my own with a guy famous enough to deserve full television coverage?

I think back to my one television appearance at a WPT final table. If you want to see two humorous clips of my action there, go to YouTube and type the words Duckman and WPT in the search box. I remember how desperately I concentrated to avoid embarrassing moves that would be captured forever on the Internet. It turned out that my WPT experience was the best poker fun I ever had, and I give much credit to my tablemates and Mike and Vince, the announcers, for making it that way.

But this televised table was different. I didn't know the players, couldn't be sure of why we were being televised, and had no idea who would be announcing the action. I decided it would look unprofessional to take notes, so I have no records as to the various hands and how they played out. I also lack precise information as to my exact finish when I busted out of the tournament. My only memory that lives on—I repressed the rest—is that my final hand of trip queens lost to a full house, which promptly and unceremoniously sent me to the rail.

"At least," I mutter to myself as I make my hasty retreat, "the French player didn't take me out." I know that will lessen the chances that my bust out will be featured in the edited version of the day's action.

I walk out of the Rio in a somber mood, feeling sorry for myself. In less than twelve hours, I have lost one tournament twice (the super seniors) and a second tournament once (the 6-handed no-limit hold'em) for a financial loss of $7,000 plus a loss of morale that is priceless. Adding to my misery is the realization that it is Father's Day and my wife and daughter are 2,400 miles away.

My only consolation: They aren't in Vegas to see me play out my personal rendition of *The Father's Day Massacre.*

CHAPTER 14

Where's a Surgical Mask
When You Need One?

In poker lingo, when someone dies people say, 'He cashed in his chips.' I was playing in a tournament when a player died with chips still on the table. They were blinded off, but not before I busted out and he made it into the money. It stings when you lose to a dead man.

One of the great things about poker is the democratic nature of the game—anybody can sit at the table, as long as he or she has enough money to play. Unfortunately, this equalitarian approach also has a downside. You have no control over who is going to sit down next to you for, possibly, ten hours or more. This has led to problems of varying severity, some so common they even have names. As examples: Armpit Arnie is your olfactory nightmare; Sam the Slob attacks your optic nerve; and obnoxious O'Neil offends your sense of decency.

Yet, in a game played at close quarters with cards and chips handled by ten different players, nothing is worse than David or Diane, Duke and Duchess of Disease. If you've played poker with any level of frequency, you know this type of person all too well. They sit down next to you and immediately begin coughing, wiping their running noses on tissues (or the back of their hands if you're really unlucky), even sneezing with no attempt to stop the germs that come hurtling out of their mouth. Then there's the guy or gal who sits down next to you wearing a surgical mask across their face. One immediate question should instantly pop into your mind: "Is this mask for their protection because they have a weakened immune system and can't breathe in the unfiltered casino air, or is it because they are sick as hell and trying not to spread whatever strain of influenza is ravaging their body?"

I don't know about you, but when I see a woman or man showing obvious symptoms of illness or wearing a mask sitting next to me at the poker table, I know it's going to affect my concentration and thus, my ability to play my A game.

TIPS AND QUIPS: TIP #5:
Angle Shooting for the Commuter

To illustrate to you how unnerving and disturbing a person wearing a surgical mask can be, I will tell you how I used to keep people from getting close to me on crowded subways and commuter trains when I travelled between New Jersey and New York for my job back in the late 60s/early 70s. I would don a large, white surgical mask and then take an empty seat on my public transport. Over 90 percent of the time, the seat next to me and across from me, if there was one, remained empty once a prospective seatmate spotted my mask as they walked down the aisle. Even in crowded trains and subways, seats near me were the last to fill, if anyone sat down at all.

If a person did sit down next to me, I could often dislodge them by simply shaking my body and moaning quietly. If that didn't work, I would administer the *coup de grace*. I would pull a pill bottle out of my pocket, take out a capsule and jam it into my mouth. At this point any would-be seatmates normally scattered like tumbleweeds in a dust storm.

My most memorable moment pulling this space-saving gambit occurred on a commuter train from New York City to Princeton Junction, New Jersey. I was sitting at a window seat with my mask on when I sensed a person sitting down next to me. Without looking over to see who this individual was, I began my shaking and moaning routine. To my surprise, my newly acquired seatmate made no effort to move. This called for my pill bottle chaser. I pulled out my drug-store-issued container and made a show of swallowing a capsule that looked like serious medicine. Even this action did not dislodge the stranger next to me.

Finally, curious how this person had the courage to remain seated next to a potential medical epidemic, I looked over to view my seatmate. To my horror, he was also wearing a surgical mask, visibly shaking, and his face was ashen-white.

I got the hell out of there as fast as my legs could move!

So, what happens? As soon as I take my seat to play in a $1,000 entry NLH tournament, the gentlemen next to me suggests I wash my hands frequently because he has some kind of bug. I check him out, and he looks bad. How bad? Well, he's sweating heavily, looks ashen and I suspect he has EMS on his speed dial.

Fortunately for the healthy among us, he busts out early, but, when he gets up from the table, he just moves a few feet away and stands there. One of the remaining players thought his immobility was the result of suddenly losing all of his chips to a bad beat, but I am convinced he was so feverish he just needed time to gather his strength and bearings to make walking out unassisted a reality.

I really feel bad for the guy and say a silent prayer for him as I dash to the bathroom to wash my hands. I'll know in a few days if my hygienic efforts are effective. In the meantime, I consider all chips and cards in play to be potential hazmat material and make a mental note not to touch my face with my hands under any circumstances.

Actually, I probably shouldn't have touched my cards at all. They weren't worth the risk. I saw more paint on the nails of the woman sitting next to me than I did in my poker hands. 7-2, 3-2, 6-2, 5-3, none of my hands, using both cards, were even adding to ten! I was folding more hands than clothes on laundry day. When I did finally receive a playable hand—A-K—I got it all in against a pair of threes and promptly saw another dream of riches and a gold bracelet crushed like trash along the highway.

I didn't wait around for the cleanup crew to throw my mangled hopes into a nearby dumpster.

CHAPTER 15

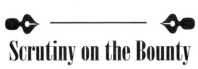

Scrutiny on the Bounty

What makes me play this poker game?
The losing always hurts the same!
Yet, when everything is said and done...
poker is so damn much fun!

Here's a solid degenerate gambler's approach to variance in poker tournaments: If you're losing one tournament after another, why not make the downward spiral even quicker and play in a turbo event, where the blinds rise dramatically faster and you are faced with playing, basically, a shove fest?

Why not?

This is exactly what I do by entering the $1,000 super turbo bounty tournament, scheduled for 11:00 AM, June 20, less than twenty-four hours after my confrontation with the "Duke of Disease" and possible exposure to some exotic microbes currently incubating in my body.

I register online, using the Bravo system to save the time and hassle involved in signing up for the tournament at the Rio. I have no need to wait in lines or carry large amounts of money, not that I have that much left. All I have to do is swipe my special Rio Total Rewards card in a machine and my seating ticket prints out in a matter of seconds. Hopefully, I'll last longer in the event than it took to register for it!

There are two ways you can win money in a bounty no-limit hold'em tournament. You can make it into the money (approximately 15 percent of the entrants) or you can knock out another player. In this particular $1,000 turbo tournament, every player begins with $5,000 in chips and blinds are raised every twenty minutes. If you knock out a player, you get an immediate $300. If you get in the money, your final money prize will be determined by how many players are still left when you either win or get felted during play.

A turbo event requires a fast start out of the box and, for once, that's what happens for me. On my third hand, I get an A-6, bet $500, and get two callers. The flop comes 3-6-9 rainbow, giving me second pair on the board with the boss kicker. I bet $500 again and get one call and a fold. The turn brings a queen and two checks. On the river, to my delight, an additional 6 hits the board, giving me trip sixes. I bet $1,000 but my opponent folds. Still, my stack is headed in the right direction, and it only gets better when I look down at pocket aces a few hands later. An opponent bets $125, and I smooth call. The flop comes K-J-8, and he bets $200. I smooth call again. The turn brings a 3, and he checks, I fire $500, and he calls. The river is an inconsequential 5. My opponent checks it to me again. I bet $1,000, and he calls. We turn over our hands and my aces easily beat his jacks.

This time I'm sitting in good shape until the third level, when I get dealt a suited A-K (known as Big Slick) in middle position and bet $800. The action folds around to the big blind who, surprisingly, goes all in, leaving me in the tank. What could he have? That kind of bet polarizes his intentions, either he wants me to call, or he doesn't. Well, that doesn't help much. A-K is a powerful hand, but its other nickname is "Anna Kournikova," because, like the tennis player, it is a beautiful sight but often loses.

What to do? I decide I've either got the guy crushed (my ace, top kicker against his ace, weaker kicker) or I'm in a coin flip situation against a pair lower than kings. I have a slightly bigger stack than my foe, so if I knock him out, I not only double-up but I also get the $300 bounty, which will cover a third of my tournament buy-in. I call. My opponent turns over a pair of fours and doesn't even have to wait until the river to trounce me. A third 4 comes on the flop, leaving mc on chip rcspirator status. Five hands later, I shove my last $600 into the pot and watch helplessly as my Kojak (K-J) loses to a pair of tens, the second 10, naturally, coming on the river.

There is no way to pull a "mutiny on the bounty" at the WSOP, so I meekly hand over my bounty chip to the guy who busted me and make my now all-too-familiar walk to the exit. A new player is already headed to my vacated seat before I even clear the room.

CHAPTER 16

❦ ——————— ❦

It Takes Three Bullets to Beat the Giant

**What happens in Vegas, Stays in Vegas...
normally, that means your bankroll.**

If you'll recall, one of the new events at this year's WSOP is called the Giant, which consists of five Day 1s on five consecutive Fridays with a low-roller buy-in of only $365, $20,000 in starting chips, 20-minute blind levels the first day and unlimited re-entries for three hours.

I had already played and lost my first entry in the June 9 Giant, and now I was taking another shot on June 23. Because I'm a night owl, I particularly liked the 7:00 PM start time for the event and felt I had a chance to turn around my latest losing streak if I could get through the first few levels with a decent-sized stack.

Things start out good, just like they had in the bounty tournament preceding this one. In an early hand, I'm on the big blind, and four people are already in the pot for $2,500 by the time it reaches me. I have an A-5 offsuit, not the greatest of hands, but certainly worth a call with the pot odds I'm getting. The flop promptly rewards my decision with an 8-5-5, giving me trips along with the ace kicker. Unfortunately, everyone folds to my $4,000 raise, but I still rake in a $10,000+ pot. A few rounds later, I get it in with pocket eights against an A-Q and hit a third 8 for a winning set and $60,000 in chips. I'm approaching $100,000 in chips when I get it all in with the only player at the table with a bigger stack than mine. As we flip our cards over, I see a dream scenario. I have A-K, he has A-J. I have him dominated. A win here puts me in serious contention to coast into Day 2—and the money. Sadly, in a "that's poker" moment, my opponent flops one of his three out jacks, and I'm felted and finished.

But wait! This is a re-entry tournament and we're only talking about $365. I quickly rationalize myself into firing a second bullet and get assigned to a new table with my fresh stack of $20,000 in starting chips. We're already in the fifth level of play ($200/$400 blinds, $50 antes), meaning that each rotation is going to cost $1,100, or 5 percent of my stack. With the short levels and already substantial blinds and antes, I'm going to have to get stacked up quickly to have a shot at bagging and getting in the money.

Chip up or ship out. It's time for some poker aggression. I don't have to wait long, going all in with A-K against my opponent's J-J. The flop comes with a king, the turn and river are rags, and now I'm sitting on $40,000 in chips. After working my stack up to $65,000 in chips over the next few levels, along comes a critical hand that propels me into Day 2 and a guaranteed cash. A woman with over $500,000 in her stack bets $27,000. She is called by a gentleman in the cutoff position. I look down at two queens and go all in. She folds, but he calls, and, since he has a stack bigger than mine, my tournament life is now at stake. He tables an A-Q against my two queens and the flop comes A-Q-10. I'm still ahead when the turn and river produces two sixes, giving me a full house and the pot. My chip stack has now swelled to over $125,000, which is what I end up bagging at the end of the day.

Now all I have to do is wait until July 8—Day 2 of the Giant—to see just how much money I am going to win. The good news: Being in the money at the Giant event marks my third cash at WSOP events, well above the one-cash goal I had set for myself at the start of my summer adventure.

CHAPTER 17

The Monster Mash:
It was a Chip Stack Smash!

Telling your wife about the Hendon Poker Mob
Internet site might not be a really great idea.

At last! The WSOP "Monster Stack" event has a reasonable entry fee ($1,500), a decent starting stack ($15,000 in chips) a good structure (60-minute levels with blinds starting at $25/$50) and is a no re-entry freeze-out.

Could this be the moment when I score back-to-back tournament cashes? Yes, I see this as a definite possibility. The Duckman is on a roll. Fear the deuces. I make a commitment to go all in if I get pocket two's. Deuces rule! I put on my Duckman poker shirt, with the deuces prominently displayed on the front, and head to the Rio for a Monster win.

I get to my table earlier than usual, which gives me a chance to size up my opposition. Two players are Asian, and that worries me. Although many Asian gamblers might not have been playing poker as long as Americans, I find them to be fearless competitors, and they are aggressive and smart.

As the clock winds down to the start of the tournament I am reminded of my twenty years spent in Singapore as lead consultant for pilot training at Singapore Airlines. One day I got in a friendly argument with one of my Asian friends about who were bigger gamblers, Asians or Americans. My friend suggested we settle the argument by visiting the closest casino to Singapore—Genting Highlands in Malaysia—and comparing the action there to what I had witnessed in Las Vegas. I was game, so we travelled to the casino, entered by the side door, considered to be better luck by the Chinese, and went to the high roller area, called the International Room.

When we got there, I asked the floor man what kind of bet I could make there in American dollars.

"$2,500, sir," was the executive's response.

I was amazed. "I thought you people catered to high-rollers," I said to the floor man. "Hell, in Vegas I can bet way more than $2,500."

The Genting executive smiled at me. "Sir," he smiled, waving his hand in an expansive arc, "I think you misunderstand, $2,500 is the minimum bet."

"Oh..." My voice trailed off. There was nothing more I could say. That answer gave me a new respect for Asian betting habits, a new understanding of just how big they did bet as I watched them wagering $100,000 and up on a single hand of baccarat!

The bottom line: It didn't surprise me that before two levels of the Monster Stack were completed, my two Asian opponents were running over the table, seemingly the newest favorites of the Poker Gods. The only time I challenged them, I bet $1,000 on J-J and had to fold when one of my Asian opponents came over the top of me all in.

It seemed that my table was the designated table of blood with player after player getting knocked out. As soon as one hapless competitor departed, another took his place, not faring any better than his predecessor.

By the end of the second break, just four hours of play, I was hanging in by the skin of my chips, and seat 7 had turned over four times, averaging a victim per hour. One Asian got moved to another table, but the remaining player had a stack of chips piled so high it was difficult to see his face. My chips, all combined together in on pile created a stack smaller than a flashlight battery—never a good sign.

I wondered if I could last to the dinner break, two hours of play away. I decided, if I was patient, I might be able to make it. It turned out I was half right, I made it halfway to dinner. At the very beginning of the final hour before mealtime, I went all in with an A-Q and got called by the big blind (not the Asian) holding pocket eights. The board ran out K-9-K-J-3. And just like that I ran out of chips, and the room.

The Monster Stack Attack had set me back, both financially and psychologically. I wondered again how the pros were able to lose tournament after tournament and come back focused and ready to play their A game the next event they entered.

I figured I needed a few days off to try and regain my mojo. My ego and my bankroll were badly battered. Of course, winning one tournament—even finishing at one final table—could turn everything around and instead of being down tens of thousands of dollars, I could be up hundreds of thousands of dollars. Such is the enticement of poker, the chance to turn a toothpick into a lumberyard. The problem is keeping a stockpile of toothpicks handy when opportunity comes knocking. And therein lies the difficulty.

My cache of toothpicks was in short supply, hardly enough to clean my teeth, let alone provide the entry fees that would allow me to clean up at the tables.

CHAPTER 18

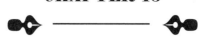

The Bullets are Flying...
My Bankroll is Dying

**I fired so many bullets I thought the
Rio was on the South Side of Chicago.**

I don't drink, but my friends that do have described what a hangover feels like after an all-night binge at their local bar.

I think that's the way I feel now. My loss at the Monster Stack the previous evening has left me with a queasy stomach and a fuzzy brain. Random thoughts, like passing fog, float through my awareness. As the day passes, I feel my senses returning to a degree of normalcy, and through it all is the disquieting feeling that I have only two-weeks left until the Main Event, and now I have a growing loss of confidence and funds to deal with.

The sensible thing to do would be to take a week off, do nothing concerned with poker, except, perhaps, study a few books on the topic, recharge my batteries around the pool and fine restaurants, and get rid of all my bad beat and poker losses by committing random acts of violence that would not endanger anyone.

Actually, Las Vegas offers ample opportunity to let off steam and reduce your hostility, specifically, the numerous gun experiences available at a price. Feel angry about getting your aces cracked? Hey, there's a helicopter you can rent where you can shoot a 50-caliber machine gun out of the passenger seat while in flight. Maybe the guy sitting across the table made a habit of stealing your big blind. Not to worry—there are gun ranges all over town where you can shoot anything from hand guns to AK-47s at targets that, with a bit of imagination, can look exactly like your blind-stealing opponent. Or maybe you're just disgusted with your own play and want to get rid of all the negative energy you've accumulated. No problem, just go to the newly opened "Axe Monkeys," an indoor axe throwing facility where you can hurl axes, like some medieval knight, at targets placed at challenging distances from where you stand.

Of course, I choose to do none of this. Instead, I go on a poker binge that starts June 25, two days after losing in the Monster Stack, and ends June 29. During this time, I play three WSOP events, the $1,500 bounty NLHE, another $1,500 regular NLHE, and even the daily $235 deep stack (non-bracelet) tournament. When not at the Rio, I decide to try my luck at Planet Hollywood, playing in two flights of the $500,000-guarantee Goliath NLHE event ($700 per entry) and the $2,000 entry Goliath $2 million main event.

After competing—and I use the word loosely, based on my performance—in these six events, I never get close to the money and end up losing $6,635 in entry fees. My only consolation is that I discover a gender-neutral bathroom down one of the corridors near the Amazon playing area and get to share restroom facilities with women for the first time in my life. I find it quite interesting to note that I make a more conscientious effort to aim carefully and not pass gas while females are occupying nearby stalls.

At the end of this debacle, I return to my rented condo and stare into the mirror, repeating the words "variance" and "that's poker" over and over like a Mantra to convince myself that winning at poker is streaky, and even long strings of losses can be followed by min-cashes, final tables, and seven-figure wins. I'm not sure I convince myself that I'll ever even bag chips again, but after taking a day off to lick my wounds, I re-enter the fray, this time, for the WSOP Crazy 8s event.

I smile at the irony of the event's name considering my current mental state of mind. After all, I must be crazy to play in the Crazy 8s event. But, hey, you have to be in it to win it, right? Sure. I register online for my seat assignment. I am disturbed to note that my one credit card is maxed out, and I need to use another one to complete the transaction. I have purposely not kept track of my financial win/loss record on the trip, choosing to do so after all my play is completed. Even so, it's not hard to realize that, even with three cashes, my $50,000 bankroll is in final meltdown mode.

CHAPTER 19

●◆ ——————— ◆●

For it's One Through Four Strikes You're in at the Crazy 8s Game

You know you're probably not a great poker player when you have to hand out 1099-forms to your opponents showing how much you paid them during the past tax year.

The Chinese consider the number 8 to be very lucky; so much so, in fact, that, years ago, a Hong Kong businessman paid half a million dollars to be assigned a license plate bearing only that number. I wonder if this is the reason the marketing gurus over at Harrah's came up with the tournament name; it also doesn't escape me that last year's winner is no other than Hung Lee, certainly in keeping with the Chinese theme.

Not being of Asian descent, nor feeling very lucky, I figure I'm already an underdog to place in this event, but I'm determined to cash.

The Crazy 8 event is geared around, obviously, the number 8. Thus, it costs $888 to enter, has eight players at each table, each with a starting stack of $8,000 chips, and awards a guaranteed $888,888 to the first-place finisher. The structure encourages reckless play with the deadly combination of small starting chip stacks, four starting flights, and unlimited re-entries for losing players. I make a mental commitment to bag using only one bullet. I begin to wonder if I can live with this restriction when the tournament director says, 'Shuffle up and deal," and my focus on possible re-entries shifts to the entry I am already in.

My first hand is a 10-4 unsuited. Not a good omen. After two orbits, it becomes clear that my table is playing tight. For the first hour and fifty-eight minutes, my stack varies between $7,000 and $9,000, within $1,000 of my starting number of chips. Then, on the dreaded bathroom hand, with blinds at $100/$200 and $25 antes, I raise to $500 with the A♦-10♦. I get one call. The flop comes A-10-6 rainbow. I check, and my opponent checks behind me. The turn brings a king. I bet $1,000, and he raises to $3,500. I go all in, and he calls.

We flip the cards over revealing my two pair against his set of kings. The river is a blank and I'm history.

> **TIPS AND QUIPS: TIP #6**
> Beware of betting hands immediately before bathroom breaks. More often than not, those that do venture a wager find themselves pissed on or pissed off.

Well, that was sudden and unexpected. Now what?

I said I wouldn't fire more than one bullet. But there was always tomorrow to consider. I could be a bit more flexible and fire a second bullet; after all, what else was there to do on a Sunday in Vegas? Then again, come to think about it, if I'm willing to bet a second bullet to try and get some traction in this event, why wait another day? There's a second flight starting in a couple hours. Yeah, that's the ticket!

Off I go to plunk down another $888 to play in the 2nd flight of the tournament. It's not long before I find myself comfortably seated at a different table with a full complement of chips ready to wreak havoc on my opponents' stacks. Which, as the 4:00 PM tournament starts, is exactly what I do. Playing an unraised 8♠-6♠ in the big blind I flop a straight on a 5-7-9 board and end up winning $10,000 when the turn and river bring a king and a jack, giving my opponents (who are both holding a king and a jack in their hand) top two pair and a willingness to call my $5,000 bet. The only reason I don't get all of their chips is the possibility of a flush (three clubs on the board) which keeps the bet sizing in a more restricted range.

Things look even better on the second round when I bet my two nines against my opponent's A-J and the flop comes A-9-7, giving me trip nines against his pair of aces. The turn is another 7, giving me a full house. I go all in and am called by my larger-stacked opponent. We show our hands, and I take great pride in spreading out my full boat. Naturally, the river brings the three-outer ace that gives my opponent a bigger full house and the suck-out he needs to score a near double-up and knock me out of the tournament at the same time.

I congratulate the winner, muttering something like "good catch" while thinking dark thoughts of a homicidal nature. I always try to be a good loser, but this failure is particularly vexing. I get away from the table as quickly as humanly possible, and find solace in an empty hallway near the back of the tournament area.

There's no escaping reality, I've shot two bullets and have nothing to show for it except a $1,776 loss. But wait! Could there be a message in this figure? After all, 1776 was when America gained independence. Maybe the poker Gods are trying to tell me something. Maybe I can gain my independence as well. But, as was the case with the American Revolution, that would involve the expenditure of bullets, in this case, an additional one.

Could I afford an additional $888? It didn't make any difference. I was in full "shit like a moose" mode, determined to recoup my entry fees and more. I hustled over to the rebuy window and purchased my re-entry ticket. I was back in play before the third level was over.

My third bullet whizzed quietly by, doing no damage. I had hardly settled in my seat before I squeezed out two red kings under the gun and bet $1,000, the next player to act raised to $3,000, followed by folds around to the button, who went all in. After the blinds both folded, it was back to me. Under normal conditions, I might have actually folded the kings to a raise and reraise, especially an all-in reraise.

But these weren't normal conditions. These were desperate conditions; worse, they were tilting conditions. I was pissed!

I looked at the button and, as I shoved my stack to the center of the table, said, "If you've got aces you deserve this." Of course, with one other player yet to act, I shouldn't have said anything, but sometimes your emotions take control of your brain, and you do things you shouldn't. As it turned out, my comment made little difference, as the guy next to me dropped out, and it was between the button and me to contest the pot.

The dealer requested we show our hands, which, as we complied, revealed my kings and my opponent's A-K. I remember thinking to myself, "Well, I got it in good; that's the best I can hope for" just before the flop produced the ace magnet, in the window, of course. The turn and river were rags, and the dealer flipped my kings into the muck. Then, as I got out of my seat again, he shoved my remaining chips to the button, who began stacking them neatly, acting like winning on a three-outer was the most natural, expected poker outcome in the world.

****

Sunday morning started like all the forty-seven days before it, with a clear, blue sky filling my room with light as I pulled back the curtains on another hot, cloudless Vegas day. I hustled into the bathroom to get ready for my Flight C appearance at the WSOP's Crazy 8s tournament. Yes, dear reader, I do readily admit that, when I arrived home on Saturday night after my three bullets, no-prize performance at the Crazy 8s tournament, I immediately went to my computer and registered online for yet a fourth shot at the event.

This wasn't some abstract game, anymore; it was *personal.* Somehow, my self-worth as a human would be determined by a simple outcome: Either I cashed in the Crazy 8s tournament or I didn't. By cunning, skill, luck, sheer willpower or some combination thereof, I was desperate to cash; every molecule in my body was programmed to produce such an outcome. Now, if only the cards would cooperate.

On the second orbit of my first round of attempt #4, I lost on my signature hand, pocket deuces to pocket queens for $1,000. It probably would have been more had not a flop of A-K and two spades slowed down my opponent's betting on the hand. I could feel the energy ebbing from my body, and the inevitable feeling of defeat well up inside my brain.

And then, things turned around. I started getting hands and winning pots. One of the biggest pots involved my K-Q against an opponent's Q-J. I won $40,000 when a queen turned, we both bet, and I won with the better kicker. Two rounds later, I was a big dog all in with my K-Q against my opponent's A-Q when a king hit on the turn and I doubled up with a three-outer. At the end of eighteen 20-minute rounds, I was finally able to achieve step 1 of my BMW approach. I was able to bag chips for a run at the money the following day.

July 3, 2:00 PM. After firing four bullets, and surviving numerous ambushes, I am through to Day 2 of this tournament. I am short-stacked but have my eye on the "M" in BMW, I want to get in the money. I sit, patiently, deciding I'll play nothing but the three top hands (A-A, K-K, Q-Q) until the money bubble bursts. The result is that I'm being blinded away like a snowball on a summer day in Florida. When the bubble finally does burst, I have just about enough chips to make one serious all-in move and still have pot equity. If I don't make a move, I have enough chips to last three more orbits. The last thing I want to suffer is a Broomcorn's Uncle and be blinded out. So, I make a move on the first hand where my two cards equal 20; in this instance, a king and a jack. I get one caller with a Q♥-10♥, and, predictably, a queen comes on the turn and it holds up.

The result? I end up finishing 550th out of 8,120 entrants for a cash of $1,949. Before I could go off and celebrate with a raucous group of supporters at some high-end restaurant, I needed to do the math. I entered the tournament four times at a cost of $888 x 4 = $3,552. My "win" of $1,949 included one of the buy-ins. Thus, it was really a win of $1,949 - $888 = $1,061. Subtracting the $1,061 from the other three buy-ins (3 x $888 = $2,664) leaves a deficit of $1,603. Thus, although I have just cashed in my *third* WSOP tournament for $1,949, it cost me $3,552 to achieve this feat!

That's poker!

No, that's *losing* poker. It's also a good reason I don't like rebuys—although I certainly will play in them—and feel that the "success" of tournament poker players needs to be called in question when we don't know how many times they entered a tournament before they actually placed in the money.

CHAPTER 20

◆—————◆

July 4th Celebration:
Dude, Scrap Those Fireworks

Poker is like sex: You're not going to
be successful if you can't get it in good.

July 4th. Fireworks! Parades! Food! A holiday that is nor-mally a highpoint on my yearly calendar. A time of family get-togethers and a chance to celebrate our blessings as Americans. This year, I am alone and failing miserably at trying to win some money in tournaments scheduled on July 3rd ($1,000 NLH), July 4th (another $1,000 NLH, this time, however, with 30- rather than 60-minute blinds) and July 5th (a third NLH for $1,500). I even sample my first single-table satellite, a $275 affair, and promptly lose that as well.

This does not bode well for the Main Event, which is less than a week away.

Despondent over my consistent inability to get in the money, let alone reach a final table, I take solace in the words of Anthony Holden in his book *Bigger Deal*. "As for the tournament circuit, I have come to the conclusion that to win one of these things [tournaments], you have to shorten the odds by playing one pretty much every week.

In fact, you have to do very little else in your life but eat, sleep, drink, and play poker, all day every day, most days of the year."

Well, I certainly hadn't done that; nor was I prepared to, for that matter.

In another section of Holden's book, he asks Mike Sexton of WPT and Party Poker fame whether he misses playing on the poker tour. The answer is both eye-opening and cautionary.

"Not really. I still get to play a few tournaments a year, but that's enough for me." Holden notes that Sexton "… remembers all too painfully the hardship that can go with being a poker pro." Sexton then goes on to state, "Everyone gets bad runs as well as good. All poker pros worth their salt know what it's like to go broke every so often. People think it looks glamorous but it's a very tough life."

Holden then observes, "For the vast majority of itinerant players on the tournament circuit, there are all the traveling and hotel expenses on top of the substantial entry fees—which adds up to an annual budget well into six figures. Only the top 10 percent get into the money in any given tournament, which means that 90 percent don't. And few are adroit enough to cover their costs in the side games."

Sexton adds a final observation. "It doesn't matter what level you play at; you still have to grind it out, to 'put the hours in.' And those hours are long and hard, often losing. I'm relieved to be spared all that…It's such a tough life. It can be so frustrating, so draining. You play your heart out, you play perfect, you get your money in with the best hand, and *still* you get beat. You have no control over it."

Gee, that sounds just like me! Maybe I'm a professional, after all. I certainly qualify according to several criteria described by Holden and Sexton, particularly the parts about getting beat, getting frustrated and getting broke.

Up to this point I had been adamant about my commitment not to check my financial gains or losses until the end of the Main Event when an official tally could be made and reported at the end of the book. I didn't want my current financial condition to affect my play. Yet, after another horrendous string of losses over the July 4th holiday, I wondered if I had actually "tapped out" and was over $50,000 in losses. A few days earlier, I had checked my safe deposit box and found only my ticket to the main event. Many of the events I had placed on my credit card, a requirement for advance sign-up on the Bravo system. I had only a few thousand dollars in my condo safe.

I checked the WSOP schedule and spotted just one additional NLHE tournament I could play, a $3,000 NLH buy-in before the Main Event. Considering my limited capital and the fact that the event was scheduled for three days, meaning Day 3 would conflict with my ability to play the finals of the Giant tournament I had qualified for weeks before, I passed on the $3,000 buy-in and prepared myself for the Giant confrontation ahead. The good news was I couldn't lose any more money in the Giant event, while the only question was, "How much would I win?"

The answer would depend on how well I performed during the event's Day 2. After that it was the Main Event and the end of my six-week WSOP adventure. The opportunity to erase all my losses and become a millionaire was a goal still in front of me and theoretically, at least, in reach.

Could I stretch that far to grab the gold ring?

CHAPTER 21

Two in a Row:
I Look in the Mirror and See a Shark

When you're winning, poker is a game of skill;
when you're losing it morphs into a game of chance.

It is July 7, 2017, and I haven't played poker for over twenty-four hours. I am beginning to get withdrawal symptoms. I look out my condo window at the mountains that encircle the city and wonder what I should do. Tomorrow is Day 2 of the WSOP Giant tournament—and that's good.

But the poker itch is strong and I don't want to wait another day to scratch it.

I go to my computer and check out the various tournaments being held throughout Vegas. One catches my eye, The Aria Classic, a one-day, $400 buy-in NLH tournament that starts at 11:00 AM and plays until there's a chop or a single winner. With 30-minute levels and $20,000 in starting chips, it seems like a good structure and a good way to keep my mind from getting too stressed thinking about the two major tournaments in my very near future. Which is how I come to be seated at an Aria tournament poker table an hour later, with my fresh stack of $20,000 chips, trying to get my bearings, having already missed two levels of play.

I wish I could tell you more about my experiences at the Aria. In my rush to leave the condo, I left my voice recorder behind, so I had no way to record my hands. Further, possibly because of my late arrival and general catch up mode, I was so focused on play that I didn't really have time to make notes on the tournament as it progressed. Which, in a way, is unfortunate, because it turns out that I actually final tabled the event, finishing 7th and winning $3,060 in the process. If you subtract the $400 buy-in, the win was actually $2,660. Well, that was an unexpected delight and put me in an excellent frame of mind for the Giant Day 2 battle the next day.

It is absolutely astounding how one victory at the poker table can rejuvenate the spirit and make one forget the horrendous losing sessions over weeks of play.

Bring on the Big Guy—the Duckman Giant slayer is ready for battle!

****

It is July 7, 2017, Day 1 of the Main Event—actually the first of three Day 1s. Most media and player attention is focused on that momentous occasion; yet for the 882 men and women who survived the first round of the Giant tournament with its 10,015 entries, the attention is on Day 2 of that event. I am one of those players.

The tournament is scheduled to begin at 2:00 PM. Yet, for reasons not totally clear, it starts 45 minutes late (the only time I have seen a WSOP event begin more than a few minutes late. Then, it takes an hour and twenty minutes to play two hands!

With so many bust outs and payout issues, the entire affair turns into a Giant mess. The confusion and delay turns out to be a backhanded compliment, of sorts, to the WSOP management team. The tournaments have been running so smoothly that the current screw-up serves to underscore how well things have been handled up to this moment. It turns out that the Giant event provides the one opportunity for the players to give the WSOP a penalty for stalling.

Finally, after two hours, normalcy is restored, and the tournament continues without further incident. Normalcy did not return, however, to the hands I was dealt. Instead, it was as if the poker gods had conspired to hit me with the deck. In a run of four straight hands I look down to see the following hole cards—A-A, K-K, J-J and A-J. Normally, this would be any player's dream scenario, but the problem with premium pairs is just that—they are only pairs and are often vulnerable to being beat by inferior starting cards that turn into two pairs, straights, and flushes.

Because all of the 882 people are already in the money, there is no bubble moment to worry about, just how far up the payout ladder a person can climb in his or her quest for riches. Therefore, I am not afraid to bet my hands. I pick up a total of $26,000 extra chips on the first three premium hands and am wondering how long this chip accumulation can continue.

The answer is very quick in coming.

On the A-J hand, I bet $1,500 and am called by one other player. We both see a J-J-3 rainbow flop. I am now thinking, "Not only are the poker gods with me, I'm going to meet them on a first name basis." I check, and the other player bets out for $35,000. I am ecstatic and resist the impulse to snap call the raise. I go in the tank for a minute. No use giving my opposition any hint of the monster I am holding. The turn brings a 7♦ and we both check. A 5♣ on the river seems harmless enough, and I wonder if I should check and let him bet or not take a chance and bet first, hoping for a call. I decide on a bet, which will reveal my strong holding, unless he thinks I'm bluffing, but is still small enough to guarantee a call and, hopefully, even a raise.

My opponent does exactly what I am wishing for; he goes all in! A sizeable number of chips joins the already ample pile in the middle of the table. I don't have quite the number of chips my opponent does, but one thing is for certain, the winner of this pot is going to be in great shape for a deep run in the tournament.

I call his all in, and the dealer says, "Show me a winner."

I flip over my A-J, revealing my trip jacks, top kicker. My opponent shows two lowly treys, giving him trip threes. I am getting ready to receive a huge shipment of chips when I notice the dealer shoving them in the direction of my opponent! It is only then that I realize that he has made a full house, treys over jacks. The two board jacks that had given me what I thought was an unbeatable hand. I readily admit I never saw the results coming until they played out before me. Even then, it took a few moments to sink in. And, once the outcome did sink in, it took even less time for the utter sense of disappointment to envelop my total being.

I really don't know how I got up from the table and walked out of the Rio—in fact, it is difficult to remember that I even did it. But, somehow, I got in my car and got back to my condo safely, totally oblivious to the heat which enveloped me like a sauna as I walked between buildings and parking lots on the 112-degree, breezeless afternoon.

I ended up finishing 586th out of the starting field of 10,015 players, earning me $1,198 and my fourth WSOP cash. Again, the math reveals that "winning" in rebuy tournaments isn't always as it seems. I had fired two bullets in the event, for a total expenditure of $730 (2 x $365) reducing my actual winning to $468 for one-and-a-half days of play.

Back in the confines of my condo, I took a chair near the window and stared at the mountains that ring the Vegas valley. Tomorrow was a day off before I played Flight C of the Main Event. Coming off the consecutive wins at the Aria and in the Giant should have given me momentum and put me in good spirits for the final, and most important, tournament of my poker odyssey; yet, somehow, the way I had been defeated in the Giant event left a bad taste in my mouth and a bad memory in my mind.

A money finish in the Main Event would eliminate those problems, of course. And I wouldn't have to wait long to begin the process of erasing those memories. My only serious challenge was to make the Main Event a Main Success in my poker odyssey.

That objective, of course, was far easier conceived than achieved.

All I could do was wait, hope, play my best, and let the cards fall where they might.

CHAPTER 22

The Gain in the Main Lies Mostly in the Pain

Chip up or ship out.

It all comes down to this. Two months of anticipation, dozens of tournaments, tens of thousands of dollars, days of blistering heat, nights of gut-wrenching beats. The Main Event is finally here, and I am seated, awaiting my first hand of the tournament!

The dealer snaps the cards off the top of the deck and sends them spinning helicopter-style to each player, and just like that, the world's most famous poker game is underway.

If you are a person who can afford to play only one tournament a year and are able to come up with the $10,000 entry fee, then I would recommend the Main Event as the tournament to choose. The structure is great, the levels are long enough, and the blinds low enough to give skillful players time to use their talents to reduce the luck factor that lurks in the lower buy-in, shorter level, small chip stack events. With $50,000 in starting chips, two-hour levels, and gently escalating blinds, a poker player can pick his or her spots to make moves without worrying about being blinded out or felted because of one mistake or bad beat. Possibly most important, the Main Event is a one buy-in per person freeze-out tournament which effectively levels the financial playing field and discourages the kind of outrageous play some people make when they know they can rebuy back into the tournament if their long-shot maneuver doesn't pan out.

Knowing that if you get knocked out of the tournament there is no recourse, that, in fact, your next shot at the money is a year away, tends to make even the most aggressive players more cautious and factors like stack size and position more critical.

I look down at my first hand and see A-K suited! I can expect to receive these two cards, on the average, once out of every 330 hands, and, showing them the respect they deserve, I bet $1,000. Current poker wisdom suggests that an initial raise should be approximately two-and-a-half to three times the big blind. Seeing that the current big blind is $150, my raise is more than double what most players would expect to see.

Yet, I get two callers.

For a year I have been telling myself how important it will be for my confidence to win the first hand I play. That was the purpose of my oversized bet, to win the pot right there and be one of the tournament leaders. Thus, I am a bit chagrined when I get the two callers on such a large raise and am now faced with the distinct possibility that my drawing hand might already be an underdog to a made hand. As seems to be the case more often than not when I hold A-K, the flop delivers a trio of low value cards, 8-4-2. Not a great flop for an A-K, but, fortunately, not for my opponents either, as everyone checks around. A 9 on the turn brings another round of checks and I start to hope my ace high might be good. A jack on the river is not what I want to see, and, sure enough, one player slides four thousand-dollar chips into the pot. I can't afford to risk 10 percent of my chips on ace high and am forced to fold, as is the other player in the hand.

The $1,000 loss shouldn't really upset me, but, for some reason, I can sense myself going on tilt, feeling I have to get my money back quickly and decisively. That causes me to make a few ill-advised calls and raises and, before I know it, I am down to $40,200. Ten days of poker play are scheduled in this tournament and I'm already 20 percent into my stack in just the first two hours of action.

I start to question my wisdom of playing the Aria tournament the day before the Main—even if I did finish at the final table. Maybe I could have better used the time to rest. Or, possibly, it was getting in the money two times in a row right before the Main Event that was encouraging me to use my bravado rather than my brain. Whatever it was, I was playing like a donk.

I really don't believe that many players can accurately predict when a person is playing his C game rather than his A game, or sense the anxiety and smell the fear of a struggling tablemate. Yet, I was sure the other players at my table could sense my discomfort, if for no other reason than mostly all of my raises and big blinds were attacked with unnerving regularity.

I felt like everyone was playing just against me and, I admit, I was intimidated.

Then, I went card dead for over an hour. At least nobody could raise me off a hand! I couldn't bring myself to call the blind, let alone any type of significant bet. After completion of the first two-hour level, I made a fast bathroom visit and then tried to settle myself down and come up with a plan go get back in the game. I decided that my goal in the two hours before the next break would be to get back to my original starting stack of $50,000.

Two minutes before Level Two was slated to begin, I returned to my seat and did a chip count to get an exact assessment of my stack damage. I was down to $31,675, dangerously close to 40 percent of my ammunition was gone.

"Well," I tried to convince myself, "if I could lose that much money, I could also win that much money back." The thought of a double-up crossed my mind. Just one such outcome and I would go from 40 percent below my starting stack to 10 percent above it. I guess that's the way poker players think when they're down. At least this poker player does.

When play resumed, I decided to be patient, bide my time and only play the top four premium hands (A-A, K-K, Q-Q, J-J). I should expect to get one of those hands about one out of every five-and-a-half table rotations. As each rotation was taking between twelve and twenty minutes, that meant I should be playing a hand between every hour to hour-and-a-half. That certainly put things in perspective!

I didn't think I could wait that long to play a hand, so I decided that, if I was in position or could get in cheaply,

I might be willing to play pots with good, but less than premium, hands.

The first test of my patience came on my first big blind back from break. I looked down at a K-Q suited, and, when it got checked around to me, I threw all of my caution out the window and raised to $900, three times the big blind. Suddenly, it was as if half of the players at the table were slow-playing monster hands. My $900 got raised to $2,000, was called *three times,* and then three-bet to $4,000 before returning to me for my action which was, of course, to fold.

"Damn!" I scolded myself under my breath, "Wait for premium hands!"

The third hour expired with no more moves from me, except to fold my big blinds and antes to my opponents' raises.

The fourth level brought $50 antes and 200/$400 blinds, meaning, if you didn't play any hands, you were losing $1,100 a round. Two rounds and $2,200 later, I was still looking for a hand I could play.

Then it came. I looked down to see two stately black kings begging for action. I didn't disappoint. With a $2,000 raise in front of me, and in the cutoff seat, I called, "All in!" and shoved my stack forward. I didn't want action. Certainly not from someone holding pocket aces or anyone holding any kind of ace at all. I had seen kings cracked too often by an ace three-outer to feel comfortable with other competitors able to draw out on me.

No, with the all-in bet, I wanted to take the pot down right then and there. The button, small blind, and big blind all folded, but the original raiser, after tanking for a short time, flipped a chip into the center of the table, signifying a call. Because he had more chips than I did, this hand is for my tournament life.

We turned our cards over. The fact that my opponent had thought about calling before making the bet convinced me he didn't have aces, and, it turned out, I was right. But he did have an ace, along with a queen. I was in good shape; I was ahead; I *deserved* a double-up. The flop produced a Q-10-7, giving my opponent a few more outs. A third queen would be a disaster. The turn was a J♦, not a good card for me. Now my opponent had a gutshot straight draw, along with the chance of catching a third queen or ace to beat me. The fact that I held two "blocker" kings made Broadway (an ace-high straight) unlikely, but the terms "suck out" and "that's poker" were created for just such unlikely outcomes when they occurred.

The dealer burned and turned the river card with much less fanfare than I thought it deserved. Nor did I think my opponent deserved the card we were dealt. It was a king, giving me a set and my challenger a winning ticket to New York (Broadway). My three kings bore me no gifts; in fact, the dealer turned them over and tossed them in the muck like so much garbage, which, ultimately, they were. There was no need to count out how many chips I owed my opponent; he had me out stacked more than 2-1.

I felt a numbness creep over my body as I rose from my seat and the dealer pushed my chips to their new owner.

Before that final hand I had, at least, some chips and a prayer.

Now, all I had was the sudden, bitter taste of defeat, the anticipation of a long trip home, and an overwhelming sense of profound disappointment.

CHAPTER 23

Money Burned, Lessons Learned, Memories Earned

*When you walk up to a gambler,
ask how he is doing, and
he says 'I'm about even,'
you're speaking with a losing player.*

At the outset of this book, I set three goals for myself:

(1) Cash in at least one WSOP tournament.

(2) Leave town with my bankroll intact or enlarged.

(3) Lose weight, hopefully twenty-five pounds.

So, how did I stack up against my objectives?

As far as cashing in WSOP tournaments, I exceeded my expectations and ended up in the money four times (six times counting non-WSOP events). I also lost weight, although it was only ten pounds, less than half way to my targeted goal. My most disheartening results, however, are revealed in my bankroll massacre. Not only was I unable to increase my funds, I ended up bleeding money like a stuck pig, until, at final reckoning, my bankroll was, like, as lenders refer to it, the Titanic—underwater.

What follows is a complete table outlining the tournaments I played, where I played them, how much I bought in for (multiple entries are added together, with total number in parentheses) and how much I won or lost. Any profit figures are reported after subtracting the cost of buy-ins.

What can you, the reader, and I, the player, learn from this data?

First, I cashed in six of the twenty-nine different tournaments I entered, a respectable 20 percent.

Second, if you count my thirteen re-entries into various events, then I actually played in forty-two tournaments with a 14 percent cash rate, more in keeping with what most pros consider a minimally acceptable rate for successful tournament players.

Third, you can cash in a tournament and still end up losing money if it's a rebuy event and your entry fees are greater than your cash prize. This happened to me in the WSOP Crazy 8s event where I "won" $1,949 but actually ended up losing $1,603 because I spent $3,552 on four $888.00 entries into the tournament).

Fourth, and most important, you can cash in 15 percent to 20 percent of poker tournaments and still lose a boatload of cash. In my case, my total tournament losses for the summer busted my bankroll: $56,059!

MY SUMMER 2017 TOURNAMENT RECORD

Tournament	Buy-ins	Profit/Loss
Planet Hollywood Goliath #1	$1,200 (2)	+$45
Planet Hollywood Goliath #9	$130	-$130
Planet Hollywood Goliath #10	$200 (2)	-$125
WSOP Colossus #5	$1,695 (3)	-$1,695
WSOP 1500 2-7 Lowball #13	$1,500	+$2,072
WSOP Giant #19	$1,095 (3)	+$103
WSOP $1,500 Millionaire Maker #20	$1,500	-$1,500
WSOP $10,000 2-7 Lowball #22	$20,000 (2)	-$20,000
WSOP $2,620 Marathon #23	$2,620	- $2,620
WSOP $3,000 6-handed NL #27	$3,000	- $3,000
WSOP $2,500 NLH #29	$2,500	+ $1,844
WSOP $1,000 Super Seniors #35	$2,000 (2)	- $2,000
WSOP $5,000 6-handed NL #36	$5,000	- $5,000
WSOP $1,000 NL #37	$1,000	- $1,000
WSOP $1,000 Super Turbo Bounty #39	$1,000	- $1,000
Venetian Deep Stack $600 NL Bounty	$1,200 (2)	- $1,200
WSOP $1,500 Monster Stack #47	$1,500	- $1,500
Planet Hollywood Goliath #90	$1,400 (2)	- $1,400

WSOP $1,500 Bounty NL # 50	$1,500	- $1,500
WSOP $1,500 NL #52	$1,500	- $1,500
Planet Hollywood $2,000 Main #96	$2,000	- $2,000
WSOP $235 Deepstack	$235	- $235
WSOP $888 Crazy 8s NL # 60	$3,552 (4)	- $1,603
WSOP $1,000 NL #63	$1,000	- $1,000
WSOP $1,000 NL #65	$1,000	- $1,000
WSOP $1,500 NL # 66	$1,500	- $1,500
WSOP $275 Single Table Satellite	$275	- $275
Aria Poker Classic $400 NL	$400	+ $2,660
WSOP $10,000 Main Event #73	$10,000	-$10,000

Don't worry, I still have my University job, where I will be returning this fall to replenish my depleted financial resources.

Scanning through my tournament performance, it is interesting to note that greater than 50 percent of my total losses came from participation in just three events. I now understand why poker pro Nick Binger said you should only enter tournaments where the entry fee is not more than 1 to 2 percent of your bankroll. In my case, to enter the $10,000 Main Event I should have had a bankroll of close to a million dollars, slightly more than the $50,000 I tucked away in my safe at the Rio!

Not figured into the tournament losses already listed are the expenses a player incurs while on the road chasing the dream. While in Vegas I spent $6,000 on lodging, $1,000 on transportation and approximately $3,500 hundred on food and related living expenses—laundry, parking, tipping, etc. Then there is the issue of my $25,000 lost income when I passed up my summer teaching opportunity to play the WSOP. All in all, my summer adventure wound up costing me just a tad under $100,000 ($91,559), a bucket list experience I deem well worth it, but not something I would want to repeat—at least if my poker performance doesn't show some spectacular improvement.

****

Are there any lessons from my poker summer that might be of value to any of you readers who might be thinking of turning professional? I would hope so. Poker is not an easy game to beat, let alone make your sole source of support. First you have to beat the rake (the casino fee charged for playing), then you need funds to tip and, most important, you have to beat your opponents on a regular basis while maintaining your interest in playing the game for the long hours (often on a daily basis) required to amass a decent income.

When I interviewed poker professionals for *Deal Me In*, they shared the same beliefs expressed by players I met at tournaments across the country. Primarily, they spoke of the freedom full-time poker provides—no boss, you determine your work hours—and the adventuresome lifestyle. But, there is a vast difference between playing poker when you want to and knowing that you have to if you want to make a living.

This difference between recreational and occupational poker is, in my eyes, clearly addressed by Barry Meadow who wrote a book, *Blackjack Autumn*, about a two-month trip he took around Nevada, playing blackjack at every casino in the state. Blackjack, properly played, has a skill component that makes it similar to poker in that the proficient player can actually win money in the long run. Of course, in the short run anything can happen including extended losing streaks, the same kind of variance bemoaned and encountered by poker players worldwide.

At one point near the end of his journey, even though he had enjoyed significant financial success in his travels, he makes this poignant observation about the life of a professional card-player:

"Far from the Bondian life imagined by the masses, in which the professional gambler is surrounded by beautiful women who throw themselves at him on a daily basis, the truth is much harsher. You play alone, eat alone, drive alone, sleep alone. And you're always scared—scared you'll lose, scared you'll be robbed...I've never quite understood these gambling books in which the writer floats airily from one comped suite to the next, Monaco one day and Macau the next, and does nothing but win. Don't these people have lives? Wives and kids? Parents? Friends? Jobs? Pets?

Don't they feel lonely? Afraid? Anything?

Anything at all?"

Please don't misunderstand my intentions, here. I am not trying to discourage anyone from pursuing a poker career—only to consider the choice from a realistic perspective. Most players will not have the disposition, skill, resources or persistence to make a living exclusively from poker income. Doug Polk, a highly successful poker professional and blogger, has produced a podcast discussing just how few people can actually carve out a living from the game when all costs are considered. It is on YouTube and entitled, "How much money do poker players REALLY have?" It was published on November 28, 2016, and runs about twenty-five minutes. I recommend you watch it.

Also, poker played recreationally for the challenge of winning and increasing your bankroll is far different than the grind it out, day after day play pursued by professionals in search of a living wage. As Mike Sexton pointed out earlier in this book, if you don't truly love poker, winning will not be enough to keep the demands of relentless play from producing burnout and, often, withdrawal from the game.

As much as I love poker, I have to admit that playing it day after day reduced some of the excitement and passion I felt when I was able to enter tournaments that were spaced apart at greater intervals, as was the case when I was not playing in the WSOP. I also found it hard to adjust to a profession where losing eight out of ten times you play is considered acceptable, professional-grade poker. I am aware that winning just one tournament during my quest at the WSOP would have sent me home a huge winner, but I still think the losing frequency would have been disturbing and detrimental to my enjoyment of the game.

Playing a tournament once a week and losing is entirely different than losing tournaments day after day. Having adequate spacing between tournaments allows me the chance to recover my hunger for the game. As a professional, I don't think I would have that luxury, making me see poker more as a job with an uncertain income stream and giving me the sense that I *had* to play, rather than I *wanted* to play, if I expected to survive.

If you, the reader, harbors the hope of becoming a poker pro, I would be pleased if you would take the opportunity to see if "living the dream" is an attainable goal. Save up enough money to give yourself an adequate bankroll to take variance out of the equation and play significantly long enough to see if you're a winner. Keep accurate records. Know if you can endure long losing streaks and bad beats and still not go on tilt. Know how much you are winning and losing, and if your win rate is increasing. Be aware of your living expenses and whether or not your poker income is able to provide you with a lifestyle that satisfies your needs. If you are married, and particularly if you have kids, study your financials to discover if you have enough steady income from poker to take care of your family and, also, enough time to be a good spouse and a good parent to your children.

And, finally, understand the critical role luck plays in the poker equation and your capacity to live with it. Poker is not chess; nor is it a sport like baseball, football, tennis or even bowling. In all of those activities, skill is the over-whelming determinant of who wins and who loses. An amateur poker player can, and has won the Main Event at the WSOP and become a poker champion. Could you imagine that outcome at a chess tournament? Could an amateur player beat a grandmaster at chess? Simply and succinctly: "No."

This is not to say that luck is a bad thing for poker. Luck levels the playing field and makes it possible for rank am-ateurs to beat the best players in the world on any given day or tournament. In the long run, the more skillful player would prevail, but that is not the issue. One reason poker is so popular is that luck can trump talent over the short run, giving the recreational player a chance to play and win against the big boys. A classic and contemporary ex-ample of this was John Hesp's 4th place finish in the 2017 main event. This recreational player, who dresses like a male peacock on full mating display and shows winnings of slightly more than $2,000 on the Hendon Poker Mob database, was actually leading the Main Event until he lost two major pots and was unable to recover.

Nevertheless, the fact that, after nine days of poker, this rank amateur was in a position to win the most sought-after poker prize on the planet says everything about skill, luck and poker's appeal to the average player.

But how you, as a player, respond to the luck factor in poker will have an impact on your overall success or failure in the game, and, for that reason, it is important to consider.

In this context, consider the observations made by James McManus, celebrated poker author and Main Event final-table finisher. These observations come by way of an email from McManus to his friend, and fellow author and player Anthony Holden, reprinted in Holden's book *Bigger Deal*. In his message, McManus provides these insights into what he witnessed while playing in the 2006 Main Event:

"Three young guys at the opposite end of my table spent the day trying DESPERATELY to get broke. Playing wild and coming from WAY behind with miracle cards. One misplayed aces on a flushing, straightening board about as bad as aces can be misplayed. He also cracked A-A with A-10. Dozens of other similar plays in the first three hours…Then one of them makes it four times the big blind in early position. I call with 9-9, button calls too. Flop comes J-9-7. Early raiser bets $2,000, I move in for $7,200, button folds, the bettor is THRILLED to call with Q-Q…and rivers a straight.

Of course, this sort of stuff happens thousands of times every minute in this town, to say nothing of the Internet. But that is my point: the luck factor is so ridiculously high that I'm really left with no other conclusion that NLHE isn't really a skill game, all things considered. I may as well be putting money into slot machines. ...I'm serious, fuckin' serious. I have to reevaluate the focus of my one and only fucking life. The best poker hand seems to stand up maybe half the time, though at my table today the worst hand rivered itself back from the dead WELL over half the time."

I suspect that once McManus had a chance to calm down and see the game from a more long-term perspective he probably reevaluated it in a more positive light, but this is what the luck factor can do to even the least-tilted, intelligent players. If you can't accept luck as part of the game and move on when hit with a string of bad beats, you will probably have difficulty surviving, let alone prospering in, the brutal game of poker.

Should you seek fame and fortune at the tables, please accept my best wishes for becoming the next breakout poker millionaire and life-long successful player.

EPILOGUE:

Don't Always Delay for Tomorrow What You Can Enjoy Today [Translation: Do Your Bucket List Before You Kick the Bucket!]

*If you choose not to live your dreams
then perhaps it's best you remain in slumber.*

There is no denying that poker has come an incredibly long way from its shady, socially-shunned past to its sparkling, socially-accepted, current popularity. The speed of the transformation is difficult to grasp. To put things in perspective, when I wrote the autobiography of WSOP co-founder and two-time WSOP bracelet winner Lyle Berman, he told me about being arrested and kicked out of Wharton Business School for playing poker in the 1960s. Fast forward to 2005, just a few decades later, and Wharton is sending a team of students to compete against opposing teams from twenty-six of the nation's top business schools, in—get this—the MBA World Series of Poker at Binion's in Vegas!

I was not part of the early popularization of poker. My passion for the game began in my seventies, around 2013.

It was my way to detox from a half century of dice degeneracy, to stem my losses and enjoy my new friends at the tables. And there were friends galore. It was amazing, really. After playing consistently for only a few weeks, the cardroom regulars would offer to make room at their table for me, even if there was a waiting list and they had to squeeze in an extra chair and play eleven-handed. Within months, my popularity soared and my mere entrance into the casino was met with invitations from friends at several tables who were anxious to enjoy my company and my cash, which I lost with alarming regularity.

The feeding frenzy was on, and I was the fish and chips main course. It took a university colleague from the finance department suggesting I hand out 1099s to my tablemates at year's end to finally make me admit that losing at poker was a sure way to gain popularity but not profit. And so, in 2013, I resolved to become a winning poker player. A short two years later, buoyed by my final table finish at a televised WPT event, I began formulating my plan to play in the biggest poker tournament on Earth and, hopefully, spear a few desert sharks along the way. Two years later that dream would become reality.

The decision to take leave of my job and risk nearly $100,000 on a bucket list dream to play the World Series of Poker was not taken lightly. All of us have dreams we wish to turn into memories. The questions become:

(1) What do we want to do?

(2) What can we do to make it happen?

(3) When do we want to do it?

My desire to spend a summer in Vegas at the WSOP is an idea of relatively recent origin, but what gave me the courage and urgency to push forth with my plan was rooted in two events that occurred over a span of nearly three decades.

I'd like to share these events with you in the hope that they will help you understand why I did the Vegas poker trip and, also, why it is important that you take the time to check as many items as possible off your bucket list, before you end up kicking it.

A Brother-in-law's Legacy

Back in the 1980s I traveled to Minneapolis to visit my sister and her husband, Shel. Shel was the typical American guy of his era. He worked hard at his insurance job, liked sports, smoked and ate a bit too much, and was a wizard at the backyard barbeque. I remember this one visit in particular because Shel had made his special honey-glazed ribs, always a cause for gustatory excess and taste bud delights.

It was a cool Sunday afternoon during early October, one of those crisp, clear fall days splashed with the color of falling leaves and the sounds of restless birds, the kind of autumn day that made you forget that the promise of a Minnesota autumn is the curse of a Minnesota winter soon to follow.

At the end of the dinner, I found that my gluttony had rendered me incapable of movement. I stretched out in my chair and, without additional food to distract me, I turned my attention to Shel and our discussion that had preceded the arrival of dessert.

Shel's 44th birthday was coming soon and he was registering his annual complaint about how he still hadn't had the opportunity to visit Las Vegas.

"I told you I'd go with you whenever you want," I reminded him. "I made the same offer last year. Are you sure you want to go that badly?" I eyed him directly, trying to gauge the level of his desire from his facial expression.

"Yes!" he said emphatically. "I've waited a lifetime to go to Vegas."

He looked convincing.

"Well, then, what are we waiting for? Let's make plans now."

Shel rose from his chair and walked over to my side of the table. "I can't make it this year," he said regretfully, "I'm up to my neck in casework."

"That's what you said last year," I reminded him.

"Okay, but next year will be different. I'll make sure. I promise you, we'll do it next year." He extended his hand. "We got a deal?"

"You're on," I agreed, and we shook on it.

The problem was, there would be no next year for Shel. He was diagnosed with an aggressive form of cancer and died before his 45th birthday.

A Visit to My Doctor

The second event that played a key role in my Vegas decision happened quite recently, just two years ago. I was sitting on the commode, reading the newspaper obits, when I noticed that more than half the deceased were born after me.

I found this unnerving, so when I spotted a doctor I knew casually at a social function, I asked him, "What is my life expectancy?"

"You've exceeded it," he replied bluntly. I couldn't be sure if he was joking or serious, but he moved off and I never had a chance to find out.

At any rate, the doctor's longevity assessment got me thinking. I didn't want to die with more dreams than memories—more "will dos" than "have dones"—so I decided, right then and there to start undertaking the activities on my bucket list.

Through the doctor's off-handed response, I discovered a new appreciation for my own mortality and the danger of taking life for granted. My thoughts turned to Shel, how he assumed he had all the time in the world when, in fact, he would live but half a normal lifetime. The fact is, death is our birthright, and there are no guarantees about when the Grim Reaper will come calling.

Shel's Legacy

Whenever I hear someone say, "I'll do such-and-such next year," I always think of Shel, and I'm reminded that none of us are ever guaranteed a "next year" or even a "next week."

Shel put off an activity he badly wanted to do because he assumed he had unlimited time to make it happen. He was mistaken.

Don't you be. I assure you, I won't be.

When it comes to undertaking an activity you really want to do, do it. That is one of the important takeaways from this book.

Some readers might see this viewpoint as being somewhat selfish and irresponsible. After all, is not the ability to postpone gratification the hallmark of being a responsible, mature adult? Yes, to a point. I'm not suggesting that a person chuck his family and job and head for some tropical paradise or casino to live out a fantasy of sun, surf, and sand. Nor am I recommending adultery, murder, or embezzlement as a means of getting what you want.

What I am saying is we need to live lives that are more than responsibility without reward. The standard phrase I am echoing here is, "We need to stop and smell the roses." We all need to find a balance in our lives between doing what we are expected to as responsible adults and doing what we enjoy doing as individuals taking time for joyful living.

There is nothing wrong with taking a break.

With taking that long-dreamt of vacation.

With saying, "It's time to do something for me."

For each of us there is a continuum of behavior that runs

from selfless to selfish behavior. When we are selfless we give too much of ourselves and expect too little from others; when we are selfish we give too little of ourselves and expect too much from others. Both ends of the continuum are unhealthy. We need to achieve a balance between doing things for ourselves and for others, between giving of ourselves, and giving to ourselves. It is this balance that creates the greatest joy of living and the greatest joy of giving.

And it is this balance that allowed me, without guilt, to embark upon the poker journey described in this book.

Did I have fun?

Absolutely.

Did you, the reader, gain valuable insights into winning at poker while being entertained and enlightened at the same time?

I hope so!

And, finally, was the journey worth it? Without a doubt. I wanted to experience, if only for a few months, what it was like to live the life of a professional poker player. On this trip, what mattered most was not whether I won or lost but that I played the game. Yes, the journey was well worth it.

And what of the future? Well, poker isn't going away. The 2017 WSOP broke its record for number of attendees, prize money and places paid. Also, the Main Event drew the largest turn-out since 2010. So, as long as the good

Lord grants me life, I will return to Vegas next year for another crack at the main event, full of hope and dreams of winning, like a baseball team thinking "World Series" on Opening Day. Hey, it took the Cubbies almost a century to win the big one; but they kept trying and finally did.

One thing is for certain, I don't, like the Cubs, have ninety-five years to win poker's biggest prize, but, as long as I'm breathing, I'll be saving up my $10,000 buy-in and declaring the words, immortalized by sports fans everywhere, "Wait 'til next year!"

APPENDIX A:

A Brief Description of
How No-Limit Hold'em is Played

No-limit hold'em (NLH) can be played with between two to ten players at a standard poker table. If the game is being played at a casino or online, a **button**, about the size of a hockey puck in brick-and-mortar games, designates, for purposes of play, who is "dealer." After each hand is completed, the button moves to the next player in a clockwise rotation.

To stimulate action, **blinds** and in tournaments, **antes** as well, are introduced into the game. These are forced bets made by the players before they see their hands. In **cash games**, the blinds remain the same and there are no antes. In **tournaments**, the blinds and antes steadily increase over time.

Play of the hand begins with each player receiving two cards face down. These are the player's **hole** or **pocket cards** and can used only by the holder of those cards. A round of **betting** then commences, starting with the player immediately to the left of the big blind and continuing clockwise around the table.

This first player has three options:

(a) **Call**: equal the amount of the big blind;

(b) **Raise**: make a bet that is at least twice the size of the big blind; or

(c) **Fold:** discard his or her cards and forfeit play for the remainder of this hand.

All bets made by players, either in the form of a call, bet or raise, are placed in front of their hands and at the conclusion of betting in the round are pulled by the dealer into the **pot**, the accumulation of all bets that will get awarded to the eventual winner of the hand. The pot is the prize that each player competes for on each deal of the cards.

After the round of betting, if there are two or more players still in the game, the dealer will turn over three cards in the center of the table. This is called the **flop**. These are **community cards** and can be used by all remaining players to make their best possible five-card poker hand. A second round of betting then takes place, with each player having the option of checking (if no bet or raise has been made before his or her turn to act), folding, or raising.

If, after the second round of betting, two or more players are still in the game, the dealer will turn over a fourth community card, known as **fourth street** or the **turn**. Players are then given the opportunity to bet again.

If, after this third round of betting, two or more players are still in the game, the dealer will turn over a fifth, and final, community card. This card is called **fifth street** or the **river**. This is followed by one last round of betting.

After this fourth and final betting round, any remaining players go to **showdown**, the final act in a poker hand, and reveal their hole cards. The player with the best five-card poker hand, based on any combination of his or her hole cards with the five community cards (including using all five cards in the middle as their best hand)—wins all the chips in the pot. In the event of a tie, the pot is split between the players who have tied the hand.

At any time during the game, if all players, except one, have folded, the remaining player wins the pot and is not required to show his or her hand. That will conclude all play in the hand. The dealer will push all the chips in the pot to the winner, gather the cards, and shuffle them up in preparation for the next hand.

During any of the betting rounds, a player in no-limit hold'em can wager anywhere between the minimum bet required to stay in the game and the total amount of chips in his or her possession. When players bet all their chips at one time, that act is known as **moving** or **going all in**.

APPENDIX B:

A Brief Description of
How No Limit Tournaments are Played

No-limit hold'em (NLH) tournaments vary widely in what they offer the player, and before entering any particular one, the prospective player should consider:

(1) The amount of money it will cost to enter the tournament—the **buy-in**. This can vary from a few dollars to a million dollars or more.

(2) Whether the tournament is a **freeze-out** (only one buy-in allowed) or a **re-entry/rebuy** event, where multiple buy-ins are permitted.

(3) If the tournament is not a freeze-out, how many rebuys/re-entries are allowed, how long into the event are these purchases allowed, and are there any **add-ons** permitted, the purchase of extra chips during tournament play.

(4) How much of your entry fee goes into the **prize pool**, the amount which will be paid out to the winning players, and how much is kept by the casino for running the event (the **house vig**) and tipping the staff? This is an important piece of information to know as the percentage of money withheld from the prize pool can vary widely from casino to casino and event to event.

(5) What are the blinds and antes, how fast do they escalate, and by what amount?
(6) How many chips will you be starting with?
(7) How long are the playing levels during the tournament?
(8) Is the event a single or multi-day event?
(9) What is the payout structure for the tournament?

To enter a tournament, you go to the tournament and/or cashier's cage and pay the entry fee. In return, you receive a **seat assignment**, your ticket of admission to sit in a specific seat at a specific table and get the opportunity to play. Upon arrival at the table, the dealer will check your entry ticket and also ask for some form of personal identification. You will then be given your chip stack and be ready to play.

Before the tournament begins, an announcer will go over certain rules and also indicate which seat gets the button. The players immediately to the left of the button will then post the small and big blind (the big blind is normally twice the size of the small blind). Once the tournament gets underway, the game proceeds as explained in Appendix A.

As players drop out, tables **break**, and if it is your table, you will be asked to go to a different table to continue playing. This is done to keep an equal number of players at each table as players bust out of play and the remaining pool of players shrink.

If you are playing in a multi-day tournament and still have chips remaining at the end of the first day of play, you will be asked to **bag** (place in a Ziploc-like container) those chips and return for play at the next scheduled session of the tournament (normally, the next day).

If you are fortunate enough to still have chips when the payout level nears, you approach what is called the "bubble." The **bubble** is the last remaining player that will *not* get in the money. Thus, if you are in a tournament that pays fifty-five players, then the fifty-sixth player remaining who busts out of play in the tournament is the bubble guy or girl. Being the bubble guy or gal is one of the most painful experiences in poker.

As the bubble is reached, the tournament director will normally call for **hand-for-hand play**, which is when each table plays one hand and then waits till players at all other tables have also played a hand. This hand-for-hand play continues until some hapless player busts out and everyone remaining is **in the money**, that is, they each have earned the minimum award level of the prize pool. From that point forward, hand-for-hand play ends and the remaining players compete to get higher up in the pay scale with the hopes of being the last remaining player— the champion!

Tournament payouts rise—you get more prize money— the more players you outlast. In large, multi-table tournaments, big money is reserved for first, second and third place finishers. To reach that level, you must first get to the **final table**, the last remaining table of players and a prestigious, and might I add, lucrative achievement in a tournament, especially at the World Series of Poker.

Because of the wide disparity in payouts between tenth and first place, and, also, because, once you get to a final table, the blinds are so high that most player's tournament lives are in jeopardy, entrants will often agree to a **chop**, a negotiation by the remaining players to distribute the prize money on a more even basis between them, with the chip leaders negotiating for the largest share and the smallest stacks a smaller share, but still, for the smaller stacks, a greater cash award than had they finished in the lower positions at the final table. On the other hand, the larger stacks receive a lesser amount than they would receive had they finished in the chip position they currently held. It is a way for all the final table players to hedge their bets.

Chopping in tournaments is a complex issue. Sometimes tournaments do not allow chopping. Other times, you risk not getting paid if a chop goes bad. Be sure to know exactly how you are going to receive your money—and how much money you are going to receive—before you make a chop agreement. In some tournaments, players will agree on a chop and then play on to determine who gets the trophy for first place. If no chop is decided upon by the final table players—the decision *must* be unanimous to be valid—then the tournament will be over when one player has accumulated all the chips that were in play. This last remaining player is the winner, or champion.

Large tournament winnings, usually somewhere over $5,000, are automatically reported to the IRS by the tournament organizers. Be sure to report these winnings when filing (you can deduct losses against your winnings, but you need to keep good records). Also, be aware that casinos often report your winnings as the total amount of money you received, which is not an accurate assessment of your "winnings." For example, if you enter a $10,000 tournament and win $10,000, the casino might well send a form to the IRS claiming you won $20,000 when, in fact you won only $10,000. If you report a win of $10,000 and the casino sends in a report that you won $20,000, an audit is not an unlikely outcome. To remedy this potential problem, you may wish to consult a tax professional who can help you in this matter.

REFERENCES

Alvarez, A. *The Biggest Game in Town.* Boston: Houghton Mifflin, 1983.

Berman, L. & Karlins, M. *I'm All In: High Stakes, Big Business, and the Birth of the World Poker Tour.* New York: Cardoza Publishing, 2005.

Holden, A. *Big Deal: One Year as a Professional Poker Player.* London: Bantam, 1990.

Holden, A. *Bigger Deal.* New York: Simon & Schuster, 2007.

John, S., & Karlins, M. *Deal Me In: Twenty of the World's Top Poker Players Share the Heartbreaking and Inspiring Stories of How They Turned Pro.* Las Vegas: Phil's House Publishing, 2009.

Karlins, M. *P$yching Out Vegas.* New Jersey: Lyle Stuart, 1983.

Karlins, M. "Poker on Twenty-Thousand Dollars a Year." *Win Magazine,* March, 1991, p. 18.

Karlins, M. "Let's Stop Making a Mockery of Tournament Poker." *Card Player.* Jan. 21, 2015.

McManus, J. *Positively Fifth Street.* New York: Picador, 2003.

Meadow, B. *Blackjack Autumn.* Las Vegas: Huntington Press, 2013.

Navarro, J., & Karlins, M. *Read'em and Reap.* New York: HarperCollins. 2009.

Polk, D. "How Much Money do Poker Players REALLY Have?" *YouTube*, July 26, 2017.

Roberts, L. "017 Marvin Karlins, Ph.D. Be the Best YOU Can Be! (Not the Best There is)." YouTube, July 26, 2017.

Sexton, M. *Life's a Gamble.* England: D & B Publishing, 2016.

About the Author

Marvin Karlins, Ph.D. (Princeton University) is a best-selling writer who has co-authored two poker books, *Read 'em and Reap* and *Deal Me In*, as well as the monster seller, *What Every Body is Saying: An Ex-FBI Agent's Guide to Speed-Reading People*. He was also senior editor and columnist at *Gambling Times/Win Magazine* for a decade and his poker articles have been featured in *Cardplayer* and *Bluff* magazine. Dr. Karlins is a senior professor of Information Systems/Decision Sciences at the University of South Florida's School of Business, earning enough money to keep his poker dreams alive.